# Brownies, Shortbreads and Toll House Cookies

# BROWNIES, SHORTBREADS AND TOLL HOUSE COOKIES

*150 delights for teas and desserts*

◆

# AARON MAREE

Angus&Robertson

An imprint of HarperCollins*Publishers*

*AN ANGUS & ROBERTSON BOOK*
*First published in Australia in 1992 by*
*CollinsAngus&Robertson Publishers Pty Limited (ACN 009 913 517)*
*A division of HarperCollinsPublishers (Australia) Pty Limited*
*25-31 Ryde Road, Pymble NSW 2073, Australia*

*William Collins Publishers Ltd*
*31 View Road, Glenfield, Auckland 10, New Zealand*

*HarperCollinsPublishers Limited*
*77-85 Fulham Palace Road, London W6 8JB, United Kingdom*

*Distributed in the United States of America by*
*HarperCollinsPublishers*
*10 East 53rd Street, New York NY 10022, USA*

*Copyright © Aaron Maree 1992*

*National Library of Australia*
*Cataloguing-in-Publication data:*

*Maree, Aaron.*

  *[Cookies, biscuits and slices of the world]. Brownies, shortbreads*
  *and tollhouse cookies*

  *Includes index*

  *ISBN 0 207 17741 4.*

  *1. Cookies. 2. Biscuits. I. Title. II: Cookies, biscuits and slices*
  *of the world.*

*641.8654*


*Photo Stylist: Karen Carter*
*Assistant Stylist: Megan Smith*
*Photographer: Andre Martin*
*Chef's Assistant: Angela Jarvis*
*Typeset in 10 pt Baskerville*
*Printed in Hong Kong*

*5   4   3   2   1*
*96 95 94 93 92*

# CONTENTS

This book is dedicated in memory of my best friend
Richard Healy.

# ACKNOWLEDGMENTS

Villeroy and Boch (Australia) Pty Ltd

John Reid, Marketing Manager, Defiance Milling, Qld

David Watson, Marketing Manager, The Good Egg Corporation, NSW

Anna Permezel, Rod Slater and James Tan, Cadbury Schweppes Pty Ltd

Jan Liddle and Paul Lawson, Glad Products of Australia

Brian Cox, State Manager, Socomin International Fine Foods, Qld

John Dart, Trumps Nuts and Dried Fruits, Qld

Mark Villiers, Marketing Manager, Bonlac Foods Pty Ltd

Pastry chefs Rene Christiansen and Gerhard Hierl, my tutors 1984–1987

Kenwood Appliances

Sunbeam Victa Corporation

Ray Doherty, Allied Packaging, Sydney

André's Party Hire, Sydney

# ABOUT THE AUTHOR

At just 23 Aaron Maree has become one of the leading pastry chefs in Australia with numerous awards and honours to his credit.

His culinary career began with an apprenticeship at Oskar's Garden Restaurant on the Queensland Gold Coast. He began as a general chef's apprentice but quickly found his real interest lay in the art of pastry making. 'Pastry is a lot more creative and rewarding' Aaron says.

Studying under German, Danish and South African master pastry chefs, Aaron became fascinated with the artistic possibilities of marzipan, fondant and chocolate.

In 1988 he won the prestigious Patissier '88 competition, his profession's highest award, competing against the finest pastry chefs in the country whilst still only an apprentice. Completing his training the same year with the Sheraton Hotel Corporation, Aaron spent the next two years travelling and working in some of the finest hotels in Europe.

He returned to Australia in 1990 to take up a position as the Brisbane Polo Club's executive pastry chef and in the same year won the Young Queenslander of the Year award in recognition of his outstanding achievements in the hospitality industry.

Since that time Aaron has continued to develop and refine his skills with the finest patissiers from around the world, winning travelling scholarships to the United States, Canada and Europe.

Aaron's hectic schedule includes lecturing and demonstrating at colleges and cookery schools, as well as writing for newspapers and magazines.

# CLASSICS

*Biscuits and cookies that have stood
the test of time and become truly classic fare.*

## CATS' TONGUES

These French cookies are long and thin – like a
cat's tongue.

*165 g (6 oz, ⅔ cup) unsalted butter, softened
210 g (7 ½ oz, 1 ¼ cups) icing (powdered) sugar, sifted
4 x 60 g (2 oz, large) egg whites
60 g (2 oz, ¼ cup) caster (superfine) sugar
160 g (5 ½ oz, 1 ¼ cups) plain (all-purpose) flour, sifted
icing (powdered) sugar, extra, for dusting*

Preheat oven to 200°C (400°F) and line baking trays
(sheets) with baking parchment. Place the softened
butter and sifted icing sugar into a mixing bowl and
cream together until light and fluffy and almost
white. In a separate, clean bowl, whisk the egg whites
until they form stiff peaks (see page 159). As they
stiffen, slowly add the caster sugar and continue
whisking after each addition. Fold the stiff egg whites
into the creamed butter mixture and then add the
sifted flour. Place the mixture into a piping (pastry)
bag fitted with a 1 cm ( ½ in) piping nozzle and pipe
7 cm (2 ½ in) lengths onto the prepared tray. Allow
5 cm (2 in) between each tongue for spreading. Bake
in the preheated oven 5–8 minutes. Remove from the
oven and cool on the tray for 5 minutes before
removing to a wire rack to cool completely. Dust
lightly with icing sugar before serving.

*Makes 36*

## CHINESE FORTUNE COOKIES

The fun of these cookies lies in being able to shape
your friends' and relatives' destinies. Create funny
or serious 'fortunes' on tiny slips of paper before
starting the recipe.

*3 x 60 g (2 oz, large) egg whites
90 g (3 oz, ½ cup) icing (powdered) sugar, sifted
45 g (1 ½ oz, 3 tablespoons) unsalted butter, melted
75 g (2 ½ oz, ⅔ cup) plain (all-purpose) flour, sifted*

Preheat the oven to 180°C (350°F). Grease well
baking trays (sheets). With the tip of your finger
mark three 8 cm (3 in) circles in each tray. Place the
egg whites into a mixing bowl and whisk until they
just begin to turn into frothy whites. Continue
mixing and add the sifted icing sugar and melted
butter. Add the flour and mix with a spatula until the
paste is smooth and lump free. Allow the mixture to
rest for 15 minutes. Place 1 ½ teaspoons of the
mixture into each marked circle on the tray and
using a small spatula or palette knife spread to fill
each circle. Bake one tray at a time in the preheated
oven and only bake for 5–8 minutes or until the
cookies begin to slightly brown around the edges.
Remove the trays and, working quickly, slide a palette
knife underneath each of the cookies to remove
them from the tray. Place a written fortune in the
centre of each. Fold in half and then in half again
over the edge of a sharp-edged object. Allow to cool
on a wire rack and then serve.

*Makes 18–24*

OPPOSITE: *above, Chinese Fortune Cookies; below, Cats' Tongues*

# AMARETTI

*Amaretti are very crisp cookies, an Italian relative of the macaroon. The mixture must sit uncovered 6–8 hours before baking.*

15 g (½ oz, 2 tablespoons) plain (all-purpose) flour
280 g (10 oz, 1 ¼ cups) caster sugar
240 g (8 ½ oz, 2 ¼ cups) ground almonds
2 teaspoons ground cinnamon
juice and zest of 1 lemon
2 x 60 g (2 oz, large) eggs whites
icing (powdered) sugar for dusting

Line baking trays (sheets) with baking parchment. Place the flour, sugar, ground almonds, cinnamon, lemon zest and juice into a mixing bowl and stir together. Place the egg whites into a clean mixing bowl and whisk until stiff peaks are formed (see page 159). Fold the flour/sugar mixture into the egg whites and gently stir together. Take tablespoons of the mixture and spoon onto the prepared tray, allowing room for spreading. Set the tray aside, uncovered, for 6–8 hours. Preheat oven to 160°C (320°F). Dust heavily with icing sugar before placing in the preheated oven. Bake until the amaretti take on a light brown colour. Remove when brown and allow to cool on the baking tray. Dust with icing sugar again before serving.

*Makes 18*

# PIPED ENGLISH SHORTBREADS

*Piping the shortbread into rosettes gives a decorative shape to these timeless favourites.*

270 g (9 ½ oz, 1 cup) unsalted butter
90 g (3 oz, ⅓ cup) caster (superfine) sugar
270 g (9 ½ oz, 2 ¼ cups) plain (all-purpose) flour
90 g (3 oz, ⅔ cup) cornflour (US cornstarch)
caster (superfine) sugar, extra, for dipping

Preheat oven to 180°C (350°F). Line baking trays (sheets) with baking parchment. Place the butter and sugar into a mixing bowl and cream together until light and fluffy and almost white in appearance. Sift together the flour and cornflour and add to the well creamed butter. Ensure that the sides of the mixing bowl are scraped down and that all the butter is mixed into the flour. When well combined but not overmixed, place the mixture into a piping (pastry) bag fitted with a 1 cm (½in) star-shaped nozzle. Pipe small rosettes onto the prepared tray. Bake in the preheated oven 8–10 minutes or until the shortbreads are just turning golden brown around the edges. Sprinkle with caster sugar immediately and allow to cool.

*Makes 30*

# BAER RINGS

*The secret of success with this recipe lies in using the correct marzipan. Look for one consisting of 66 per cent almonds and 34 per cent sugar.*

330 g (11 ½ oz, 1 ⅓ cups) unsalted butter
150 g (5 oz) marzipan (see page 160)
150 g (5 oz, 1 cup) icing (powdered) sugar, sifted
1 x 60 g (2 oz, large) egg
450 g (16 oz, 3 ½ cups) plain (all-purpose) flour, sifted
juice and zest of 1 lemon

Preheat oven to 180°C (350°F). Line baking trays (sheets) with baking parchment. Place the butter, marzipan and icing sugar into a mixing bowl and cream together until light and fluffy. Add the egg and mix well. Fold through the sifted flour and the lemon juice and zest. Place the mixture into a piping (pastry) bag fitted with a 1 cm (½ in) star-shaped nozzle and pipe 5 cm (2 in) rings onto the prepared trays. Bake in the preheated oven 10–12 minutes or until lightly golden brown and allow to cool on the trays.

*Makes 24*

OPPOSITE: *above left, Piped English Shortbreads; above right, Amaretti; below, Baer Rings*

# ALMOND MOCCA BISCUITS

A *perfect blend of coffee and almonds. Only to be served with the finest percolated coffee or brewed tea.*

*180 g (6 ½ oz, 1 ½ cups) plain (all-purpose) flour, sifted*
*45 g (1 ½ oz, 3 tablespoons) caster (superfine) sugar*
*120 g (4 oz, ½ cup) unsalted butter*
*60 g (2 oz, ½ cup) ground almonds*
*1 x 60 g (2 oz, large) egg yolk*
*15 g (½ oz, 3 tablespoons) instant coffee granules dissolved in*
*25 ml (1 fl oz, 2 tablespoons) boiling water*
*24-30 whole almonds blanched (skinned)*
*1 quantity egg wash (see page 156)*

Place the sifted flour into a mixing bowl with the sugar and butter and, with your fingertips, crumb the mixture together until it resembles fine bread-crumbs. Add to this the ground almonds, egg yolk and the dissolved coffee. Continue mixing until a soft dough is formed. Remove from the mixing bowl, cover with plastic (cling) wrap and refrigerate for 1 hour. Preheat the oven to 180°C (360°F). Line baking trays (sheets) with baking parchment. Work the dough on a lightly floured surface until it is soft enough to roll. Roll the dough to 1 cm (½ in) in thickness and then using a fluted round cookie cutter (5 cm (2 in) in diameter) cut out rounds. Place the cookies onto the prepared tray. Brush each lightly with egg wash. Press a whole almond into the top of each cookie. Bake in the preheated oven 10–12 minutes.

*Makes 36*

# ALMOND TUILES

A *tuile is a thin, crisp cookie that is shaped into a curve while still warm. Tuile is French for tile – a reference to the roof-tile shape of the baked cookies. If you shape the tuile over a cup instead of the traditional rolling pin, you can use it as a dessert biscuit.*

*120 g (4 oz, ¾ cup) icing (powdered) sugar*
*120 g (4 oz, 1 cup) plain (all-purpose) flour*
*3 x 60 g (2 oz, large) egg whites*
*90 g (3 oz, ⅓ cup) unsalted butter, melted*
*150 g (5 oz, 1 ⅓ cups) flaked almonds, for decoration*

Preheat oven to 180°C (350°F). Lightly grease baking trays (sheets). Sift together the icing sugar and the flour into a bowl and then add the lightly whisked egg whites. Stir until well mixed and no lumps of dry ingredients are present. Allow mixture to sit uncovered for 5 minutes. Pour the melted butter over the top of the mixture and stir until well mixed and a smooth paste has formed. Allow to rest for a further 5 minutes. Take a dessertspoonful of the mixture and place onto the prepared tray, spreading into a large circle using the back of the spoon. Spread very thinly and sprinkle a few flaked almonds on the top of each tuile. Bake in the preheated oven 8–10 minutes or until the tuiles are just turning golden brown around the edges. (Depending on their thickness the tuiles may take more or less time.) Remove the tray from the oven and, very carefully, using a flat clean palette knife or spatula, remove each tuile quickly before it sets hard. Press over a rolling pin or any utensil which will give a curved shape. Allow to cool over the rolling pin and then store in an airtight container until required.

*Makes 12–18*

OPPOSITE: *above, Almond Mocca Biscuits; below, Almond Tuiles*

# COCONUT TUILES

*The mixture for this recipe is stored in the refrigerator for 24 hours before baking. You can keep it covered in the refrigerator for up to a week before using.*

*3 x 60 g (2 oz, large) eggs, lightly beaten*
*180 g (6 ½ oz, 1 cup) icing (powdered) sugar, sifted*
*180 g (6 ½ oz, 2 cups) desiccated (shredded) coconut*
*icing (powdered) sugar, extra for dusting*

Place the lightly beaten eggs, the sifted icing sugar and the coconut into a mixing bowl and mix until all ingredients are well combined. Cover the mixture with plastic (cling) wrap and leave to sit in the refrigerator for 24 hours, so the coconut becomes moist.

Preheat the oven to 180°C (350°F). Grease baking trays (sheets). When ready to use, stir the mixture lightly to ensure there is no liquid at the base of the bowl. Take a heaped teaspoon of the mixture and roll into a ball. Place onto the prepared tray. Using a fork constantly dipped into cold water, press out the balls until they form a 5 cm (2 in) circle.

Bake in the preheated oven for 5–8 minutes or until the edges are a light golden brown. Remove quickly from the tray using a spatula or carefully slide a palette knife under each tuile. Press the tuiles over a rolling pin or any utensil which will give a curved shape. Allow to cool and set over the rolling pin. Then either dust with icing sugar and serve or place carefully into an airtight container for later use.

*Makes 12–18*

# GALETTES ALMONDINE

*As the name suggests, galettes originated in France.*

*300 g (10 ½ oz, 2 ½ cups) plain (all-purpose) flour*
*120 g (4 oz, ¾ cup) icing (powdered) sugar*
*60 g (2 oz, ½ cup) ground almonds*
*150 g (5 oz, ⅔ cup) unsalted butter*
*1 x 60 g (2 oz, large) egg, lightly beaten*
*1 tablespoon water*

### TOPPING
*2 x 60 g (2 oz, large) egg whites*
*270 g (9 ½ oz, 1 ¾ cup) icing (powdered) sugar*
*150 g (5 oz, 1 ⅓ cup) slivered almonds*

Line baking trays (sheets) with baking parchment. Place the flour, icing sugar, almonds and butter into a bowl and lightly crumb the butter through the other ingredients until the mixture resembles coarse breadcrumbs. Add the lightly beaten egg and the water and work the mixture to a dough. Wrap in plastic (cling) wrap and place in the refrigerator for 30 minutes. Preheat oven to 180°C (350°F). Remove the dough and knead until it is ready to roll. Roll on a lightly floured surface to ½ cm (⅛ in) in thickness. Using a 5 cm (2 in) diameter round cookie cutter, cut out discs of pastry and place directly onto the prepared trays. Spoon, pipe or spread a small amount of the topping mixture over the disks. Bake in the preheated oven 8–12 minutes or until lightly golden brown. Remove and cool on a wire rack.

### TOPPING
Lightly whisk the egg whites to a soft foam. Slowly add the icing sugar, whisking continuously until mixture forms a thick paste. Lastly add the almonds. Allow to rest 5 minutes before using. Excess topping may be stored in the refrigerator for up to 10 days.

*Makes 36*

OPPOSITE: *above, Galettes Almondine; below, Coconut Tuiles*

# BAKLAVA

Usually served as a dessert, this Greek tradition is today becoming popular in lunchboxes around the globe.

*300 g (10 oz, 1 ¼ cup) butter, melted*
*500 g (1 lb 1 ½ oz) filo pastry sheets*

### FILLING
*60 g (2 oz, ¼ cup) caster (superfine) sugar*
*210 g (7 ½ oz, 1 ¾ cups) macadamia (Queensland) nuts,*
*finely chopped*
*30 g (1 oz, ¼ cup) ground hazelnuts*
*90 g (3 oz, ¾ cup) ground almonds*
*1 teaspoon ground cinnamon*
*90 g (3 oz, 1 cup) desiccated (shredded) coconut*

### SYRUP
*300 ml (10 ½ fl oz, 1 ¼ cups) water*
*360 g (12 ½ oz, 1 ¾ cups) caster (superfine) sugar*
*125 ml (4 ½ fl oz, ½ cup) white wine*
*100 ml (3 ½ fl oz, ⅓ cup) dark rum*
*2 teaspoons ground cinnamon*
*zest of 3 oranges*
*2 tablespoons clear honey*

Preheat oven to 160°C (320°F). Grease well a 30 cm x 28 cm x 5 cm (12 in x 11 in x 2 in) baking tray (sheet). Carefully open out the sheets of filo pastry and cut in half crossways. Stack the sheets on top of each other and keep covered with a damp cloth when not in use. Place the sheets onto the base of the tray, layering until the layer is 2mm (⅛ in) thick, buttering every second sheet. After every 10–12 sheets of filo, sprinkle the nut mixture evenly and gently over the pastry. Continue to layer and butter the remaining filo pastry until all the pastry and filling has been used up. Brush the top well with any remaining melted butter. With a sharp knife cut into 5 cm (2 in) squares or diamond shapes. Bake in the preheated oven 1 hour. Remove from the oven and pour the cold syrup evenly over the top. Allow to cool completely and then run a knife through marked slices and remove from tray.

### FILLING
Mix together the sugar, nuts, cinnamon and coconut in a bowl.

### SYRUP
Place all the ingredients in a saucepan and bring to the boil. Reduce the heat and allow to simmer for 15 minutes. Set aside to cool.

*Makes 12–18*

**STEP ONE:** *Place sheets onto the base of the tray layering until the layer is 2 mm (⅛ in) thick, buttering every second sheet.*

**STEP TWO:** *After every 10–12 sheets of filo, sprinkle the nut mixture evenly and gently over the pastry.*

**STEP THREE:** *Pour the topping over the baked and cut baklava.*

# GINGERBREAD

This recipe is a perfect base for a gingerbread house or for making Christmas decorations. Cut the gingerbread into decorative shapes and, after baking, make a small hole in the bread to thread with cotton and hang on the tree.

270 g (9 ½ oz, 2 ¼ cups) plain (all-purpose) flour
225 g (8 oz, 2 cups) dry cake crumbs
90 g (3 oz, ⅓ cup) unsalted butter, softened
90 g (3 oz, ⅓ cup) caster (superfine) sugar
1 heaped teaspoon mixed spice (see page 161)
2 heaped teaspoons ground ginger
180 g (6 ½ oz, ½ cup) golden syrup (light treacle)
2 heaped teaspoons baking powder
1 x 60 g (2 oz, large) egg

Place all ingredients into a mixing bowl and mix until a dough is formed. Knead the dough lightly, and then wrap in plastic (cling) wrap and place in the refrigerator for 1 hour. Preheat oven to 175°C (345°F). Lightly grease baking trays (sheets). Remove the dough from the refrigerator and knead lightly until ready to roll. Roll out on a lightly floured surface to a thickness of 3–4 mm (⅛ in). Cut the dough into any desired shape with fancy cookie cutters. Place the gingerbread shapes onto the prepared tray and bake in the preheated oven 10–12 minutes. Allow to cool on the trays before removing. Decorate with icing if desired.

*Makes 25–30*

# KOURAMBIETHES

A Greek classic. The cookie should be completely lost in its dusting of icing sugar.

210 g (7 ½ oz, 1 cup) butter
150 g (5 oz, 1 cup) icing (powdered) sugar, sifted
1 x 60 g (2 oz, large) egg
1 x 60 g (2 oz, large) egg yolk
360 g (12 ½ oz, 3 cups) plain (all-purpose) flour
1 ½ teaspoons baking powder
1 teaspoon ground cinnamon
270 g (9 ½ oz, 2 ½ cups) hazelnuts, finely chopped
icing (powdered) sugar, extra

Preheat oven to 160°C (320°F). Grease baking trays (sheets). Place the butter and sugar into a mixing bowl and cream together until light, white and fluffy. Beat in the egg and egg yolk. Sift the flour with the baking powder and cinnamon and mix lightly into the butter mixture together with the chopped hazelnuts. Take tablespoon-sized amounts of the dough and roll into balls. Place on the prepared tray. Bake in the preheated oven 15–20 minutes, or until pale golden. Cool. While still barely warm, dust heavily with icing sugar. Cool and store in an airtight container. Roll in icing sugar again before serving.

*Makes 26*

# NERO ROSETTES

An outrageously rich treat of which Nero himself would be proud.

300 g (10 ½ oz, 1 ¼ cups) unsalted butter
45 g (1 ½ oz, ⅓ cup) cocoa powder
150 g (5 oz, 1 cup) icing (powdered) sugar
1 x 60 g (2 oz, large) egg
390 g (13 ½ oz, 3 cups) plain (all-purpose) flour
juice and zest of 1 lemon
melted dark (plain or semi-sweet) chocolate (see page 160)

Preheat the oven to 180°C (350°F). Line baking trays (sheets) with baking parchment. Place the butter, cocoa and icing sugar into a mixing bowl and cream together until light and fluffy. Add the egg and mix well. Fold through the sifted flour and the lemon juice and zest. Place the mixture into a piping (pastry) bag fitted with a 1 cm (½ in) star-shaped piping nozzle and pipe small rosettes onto the prepared trays. Bake in the preheated oven 10–12 minutes and allow to cool on the trays. Turn the rosettes upside down and dip the base of each into the melted chocolate. Decorate the chocolate by running a fork through it lightly before placing in the refrigerator to set.

*Makes 36*

OPPOSITE: *above left, Nero Rosettes; above right, Kourambiethes; below, Gingerbread*

# PALETS DE DAME

*An essential recipe for the repertoire of any self-respecting pastry chef. It is important to grease and flour the baking tray well.*

*3 x 60 g (2 oz, large) egg whites*
*90 g (3 oz, ½ cup) icing (powdered) sugar*
*45 g (1 ½ oz, 3 tablespoons) unsalted butter, melted*
*75 g (2 ½ oz, ⅔ cup) plain (all-purpose) flour*

Preheat oven to 175°C (345°F). Grease well baking trays (sheets), and dust each with flour. With your finger mark three 7 cm (2 ½ in) circles on each of the floured trays.

Place the egg whites into a mixing bowl and whisk until they just begin to turn frothy. Continue mixing and add the sifted icing sugar and melted butter. Add the flour and mix with a spatula until the paste is smooth and lump free. Allow the mixture to rest for 15 minutes.

Place 1 heaped teaspoon of the mixture into each marked circle on the tray and using a small spatula or palette knife spread the mixture so that it fills the circle. Bake one tray at a time in the preheated oven and only bake for 5–8 minutes or until the cookies begin to slightly brown around the edges. Remove the trays and, working very quickly, slide a palette knife underneath each cookie and place on a wire rack to cool.

*Makes 18*

# JAPONAISE ROUNDS

*A delicious adaptation of the classic cake.*

*5 x 60 g (2 oz) egg whites*
*1 teaspoon cream of tartar*
*120 g (4 oz, ½ cup) caster (superfine) sugar*
*60 g (2 oz, ½ cup) ground almonds*
*60 g (2 oz, ⅔ cup) desiccated (shredded) coconut*
*15 g (½ oz, 2 tablespoons) plain (all-purpose) flour*
*120 g (4 oz, ½ cup) caster (superfine) sugar, extra*
*210 g (7 oz, ⅔ cup) strawberry jam*
*1 quantity quick no-fuss buttercream (see page 154)*
*210 g (7 ½ oz, 2 cups) cake or biscuit (cookie) crumbs finely ground or sifted*
*210 g (7 ½ oz) fondant glaze (see page 155)*

Preheat oven to 125°C (255°F). Line baking trays (sheets) with baking parchment. Place the egg whites in a mixing bowl with the cream of tartar and whisk until it begins to form stiff peaks (see page 159). Slowly begin adding the sugar, continuing to whisk. When all the sugar has been added and a stiff meringue has formed, add the ground almonds, coconut, flour and extra sugar, mixing until completely combined with the meringue mixture. Place into a piping (pastry) bag, fitted with a 1 cm (½ in) plain piping nozzle, and pipe small discs of mixture onto the prepared trays. Each disc should not be any larger than 5 cm (2 in) in diameter. Bake in the preheated oven 20–30 minutes or until each disc is brown and firm. As soon as they are removed from the oven, cut each disc with a 5 cm (2 in) diameter plain round cookie cutter so that each is even and clean cut. Allow to cool.

Each finished Japonaise Round requires two of the baked discs. Place a small amount of jam on the base of one disc and then pipe buttercream around the edge. Place another disc on top and then cover the sides and top of the joined discs with buttercream. When covered roll in either cake or biscuit crumbs. Melt the fondant over a saucepan of hot water. Place a small amount into a piping (pastry) bag and pipe a small dot of fondant in the centre of each Japonaise Round. Serve immediately.

*Makes 28*

# BRANDY SNAPS

*Wafer-thin and crispy – always sure to please.*

*180 g (6 ½ oz, ¾ cup) caster (superfine) sugar*
*180 g (6 ½ oz, ½ cup) golden syrup (light treacle)*
*90 g (3 oz, ⅓ cup) unsalted butter*
*90 g (3 oz, ¾ cup) plain (all-purpose) flour*

Place the sugar, golden syrup and butter into a sauce-pan and place over low heat. Allow the butter to melt and mix into all the other ingredients, but do not allow to boil. Remove from the heat. Add the flour and stir with a wooden spoon until well mixed. Pour the mixture into a container and refrigerate for 1–2 hours or until mixture is quite cool and firm.

Preheat oven to 180°C (360°F) and lightly grease baking trays (sheets). Take small teaspoonfuls of the firm mixture at a time and roll into small balls. Place each ball onto the prepared tray leaving plenty of room between each for spreading. When the tray is full, dip your fingers into cold water and flatten the balls.

Bake in the preheated oven 5–8 minutes or until all of the Brandy Snaps are bubbling and have coloured slightly. Remove from the oven and allow to cool slightly and firm for 1 minute. Peel them from the tray carefully using a knife or spatula and roll each one quickly around a cylindrical object with a diameter wider than a wooden spoon. Allow to cool around the mould. When cold, slide from the mould and either leave plain or fill with freshly whipped cream.

*Makes 24–36*

**STEP ONE:** *Peel the cooked brandy snap carefully from the tray.*

**STEP TWO:** *Roll each one around a cylindrical object and allow to set.*

# ZITRON

A *distinctive Swiss pastry with a lemon butter filling.*

300 g (10 ½ oz, 2 ½ cups) plain (all-purpose) flour
150 g (5 oz, 1 cup) icing (powdered) sugar
30 g (1 oz, ¼ cup) ground almonds
150 g (5 oz, ⅔ cup) unsalted butter
1 x 60 g (2 oz, large) egg
1 tablespoon water

### LEMON BUTTER
3 x 60 g (2 oz, large) eggs
zest and juice of 2 lemons
120 g (4 oz, ½ cup) caster (superfine) sugar
240 g (8 ½ oz, 1 cup) unsalted butter

### ICING
180 g (6 ½ oz, 1 cup) icing (powdered) sugar, sifted
2 tablespoons lemon juice
1–2 drops yellow food colouring
120 g (4 oz) dark (plain or semi-sweet) chocolate, melted (see page 160)

Line baking trays (sheets) with baking parchment. Place the flour, icing sugar, almonds and butter into a bowl and lightly crumb the butter through the other ingredients until the mixture resembles coarse breadcrumbs. Add the lightly beaten egg and the water and work to a dough. Wrap in plastic (cling) wrap and place in the refrigerator for 30 minutes. Preheat oven to 180°C (350°F).

Remove the dough and knead until ready to roll. Roll on a lightly floured surface to 2–3 mm (⅛ in) in thickness. Using a 5 cm (2 in) diameter round cookie cutter cut out two discs of dough for each Zitron and place directly onto the prepared trays. Bake in the preheated oven 8–12 minutes or until lightly golden brown. Remove and cool on a wire rack.

### LEMON BUTTER
Whisk the eggs very well in a mixing bowl. Add the lemon, sugar and butter to the eggs and stir. Place the bowl over a pot of boiling water and whisk continuously until the mixture becomes thick (15–20 minutes). Allow to cool, then refrigerate for 1 hour.

### ICING
Place the icing sugar and lemon juice together in a bowl and mix until smooth and lump free. Stir in several drops of yellow colour but keep it to a pastel shading.

### TO ASSEMBLE
Dip the tops of half the discs into the icing mixture and allow to set on a wire rack. Spread a small amount of the lemon butter on the remaining discs (these will form the base). Place one of the iced cookies on top of the base and press lightly together. Place the melted chocolate in a piping (pastry) bag and pipe a decorative Z on top of each cookie. Allow to set and harden before serving.

*Makes 18*

**STEP ONE:** *Place one of the iced cookies on top of the base and press together.*

**STEP TWO:** *Pipe a decorative Z on the top of each cookie.*

# SABLES

This is a French adaptation of English and Scottish shortbread, introduced to Europe during the Crusades. 'Sablé' means 'sand', a reference to the delicate, crumbly texture.

240 g (8 ½ oz, 2 cups) plain (all-purpose) flour
120 g (4 oz, ¾ cup) icing (powdered) sugar
pinch salt
180 g (6 ½ oz, ¾ cup) unsalted butter
juice and zest of 1 lemon
caster (superfine) sugar for rolling
apricot jam

Sift the flour, icing sugar and salt into a bowl and add the butter. Using your fingertips, crumb the butter through the dry ingredients until the mixture resembles fresh breadcrumbs. Add the lemon juice and zest and work the mixture into a dough. Divide the dough into three even pieces and roll each piece into a sausage shape 2 cm (¾ in) thick. Sprinkle the caster sugar evenly over the work surface. Roll the sausage shapes in the caster sugar. Wrap each roll carefully in plastic (cling) wrap and freeze for 2–3 hours.

Preheat oven to 200°C (400°F). Line baking trays (sheets) with baking parchment. Remove the dough from the freezer and roll in the sugar once more before cutting the sausage shapes into even 3 mm (⅛ in) rounds. Place each round onto the prepared tray. Pipe a small dot of apricot jam onto the centre of each. Bake in the preheated oven 8–10 minutes or until the edges are just turning golden brown. Remove immediately and cool on the tray.

*Makes 48*

# NUT BEAN SQUARES

A superb combination of dried fruit, almonds, spices and lemon.

150 g (5 oz, 1 ¼ cups) plain (all-purpose) flour
105 g (3 ½ oz, ⅓ cup) caster (superfine) sugar
75 g (2 ½ oz, ⅔ cup) ground almonds
105 g (3 ½ oz, ⅓ cup) unsalted butter, cut into small pieces
1 x 60 g (2 oz, large) egg, lightly beaten
25 ml (1 fl oz, 2 tablespoons) milk
125 g (4 ½ oz, ⅓ cup) redcurrant jam

FILLING
150 g (5 oz, 1 ⅓ cups) ground almonds
150 g (5 oz, ⅔ cup) caster (superfine) sugar
75 ml (2 ½ fl oz, ¼ cup) milk
75 g (2 ½ oz, ⅓ cup) mixed (candied) peel
75 g (2 ½ oz, ⅓ cup) currants
75 g (2 ½ oz, ¼ cup) unsalted butter, melted
1 tablespoon ground cinnamon
zest and juice 1 lemon
1 x 60 g (2 oz, large) egg

powdered drinking chocolate or cocoa mixed with icing (powdered) sugar for dusting

Preheat oven to 200°C (400°F). Grease well the base and sides of an 18 cm x 28 cm x 2 cm (7 in x 11 in x ¾ in) baking tray (sheet) with butter. Place the flour, sugar and ground almonds in a bowl and mix lightly. Add the butter and very lightly rub into the dry ingredients until the mixture resembles fresh breadcrumbs. Add the egg and milk to make a soft dough. Using lightly floured hands press the mixture into the greased tray. Spread the top of the dough with redcurrant jam. Pour the filling on top. Bake in the preheated oven 25–30 minutes or until firm to the touch. When cool dust with the powdered drinking chocolate or cocoa mixed with icing sugar and cut into squares.

FILLING
Place all the ingredients into a bowl and mix thoroughly.

*Makes 18*

OPPOSITE: *above, Sablés; below, Nut Bean Squares*

# CARAC

*An exquisite pastry created by the master confectioners of Switzerland.*

*450 g (16 oz, 3 ½ cups) plain (all-purpose) flour, sifted*
*210 g (7 ½ oz, 1 ¼ cups) icing (powdered) sugar, sifted*
*270 g (9 ½ oz, 1 cup) unsalted butter*
*1 x 60 g (2 oz, large) egg*

GANACHE FILLING
*150 ml (5 fl oz, ⅔ cup) cream (single, light)*
*30 g (1 oz, 2 tablespoons) unsalted butter*
*300 g (10 ½ oz) dark (plain or semi-sweet) chocolate, melted*
*(see page 160)*

ICING GLAZE
*180 g (6 ½ oz, 1 cup) icing (powdered) sugar, sifted*
*2 tablespoons milk*
*1–2 drops green food colouring*

*dark (plain or semi-sweet) chocolate, melted*

Place the sifted flour and icing sugar into a bowl and, using your fingertips, lightly crumb the butter through the dry ingredients until the mixture resembles fresh breadcrumbs. Add the egg and continue mixing to a soft dough. Wrap the dough in plastic (cling) wrap and refrigerate for 1 hour.

Preheat the oven to 200°C (400°F). Lightly grease baking trays (sheets).

On a lightly floured surface roll the dough out to 3–4 mm (¼ in) in thickness and cut two rounds for each Carac with a 5 cm (2 in) diameter plain round cookie cutter . Bake in the preheated oven 8–10 minutes or until lightly browned on the edges. Allow to cool on the tray.

GANACHE FILLING
Place the cream in a small saucepan with the butter and bring to the boil. Add the melted chocolate to the boiled mixture and stir until a smooth, rich dark chocolate cream is formed. Place in the refrigerator to firm.

ICING GLAZE
Place the sifted icing sugar in a bowl and mix in the milk to make a thin icing. Add one or two drops of green food colouring to give a subtle colour.

TO ASSEMBLE
Divide the baked rounds into two even piles; half will form the base of the Carac, the other the top.

Take the tops and dip each one into the green icing. Allow to set. Take the ganache from the refrigerator when firm and place into a piping (pastry) bag fitted with a ½ cm (¼ in) diameter plain nozzle. Pipe a small amount of ganache onto the bases. Press the tops and bottoms together. To finish, pipe a small dot of melted chocolate into the centre of each top.

*Makes 12–18*

**STEP ONE:** *Pipe a small amount of ganache onto the Carac bases. Press the tops and bases together.*

**STEP TWO:** *Pipe a small dot of chocolate onto the centre of the green iced round.*

# RUSSIAN SQUARES

*Simple but full of flavour, this bar captures the best traditions of Russian cooking.*

*105 g (3 ½ oz, ¾ cup) plain (all-purpose) flour*
*45 g (1 ½ oz, ¼ cup) icing (powdered) sugar*
*60 g (2 oz, ¼ cup) unsalted butter*
*1 x 60 g (2 oz, large) egg*

FILLING
*180 g (6 oz, ¾ cup) unsalted butter*
*120 g (4 oz, ½ cup) caster (superfine) sugar*
*2 x 60 g (2 oz) egg yolks*
*120 g (4 oz, 1 cup) plain (all-purpose) flour*
*60 g (2 oz, ½ cup) ground rice (coarse rice flour)*
*1 ½ teaspoons baking powder*
*60 g (2 oz, ⅓ cup) sultanas (golden raisins)*
*60 g (2 oz, ⅓ cup) currants*
*60 g (2 oz, ⅓ cup) glacé (candied) cherries, chopped*

Preheat oven to 175°C (345°F). Grease and line an 18 cm x 28 cm x 2 cm (7 in x 11 in x ¾ in) baking tray (sheet) with baking parchment. Place the flour and sugar in a bowl. Add the butter and lightly rub into the flour until mixture resembles dry breadcrumbs. Add the egg and mix thoroughly. Turn the dough onto a lightly floured surface and knead lightly. Press into the prepared tray. Spread the filling over the base. Bake in the preheated oven 25–30 minutes or until firm to the touch. When baked, cool and cut into squares.

FILLING
Place the butter and sugar in a mixing bowl and cream together until light and fluffy. Add the eggs and mix well. Add the flour, ground rice and baking powder and combine well. Lastly fold through the dried and glacé fruits.

*Makes 18*

# SHREWSBURY SHORTBREADS

*Serve warm with tea or coffee.*

*450 g (16 oz, 3 ½ cups) plain (all-purpose) flour, sifted*
*225 g (8 oz, 1 ½ cups) icing (powdered) sugar, sifted*
*270 g (9 ½ oz, 1 cup) unsalted butter*
*1 x 60 g (2 oz, large) egg*
*redcurrant (or similar sour berry) jam*
*icing (powdered) sugar, extra, for dusting*

Place the sifted flour and icing sugar into a bowl and using your fingertips, lightly rub the butter through the dry ingredients until the mixture resembles fresh breadcrumbs. Add the egg and continue mixing to a soft dough. Wrap the dough in plastic (cling) wrap and refrigerate for 1 hour.

Preheat the oven to 200°C (400°F). Lightly grease baking trays (sheets). Cut two rounds for each Shrewsbury with a 5 cm (2 in) diameter fluted round cookie cutter. Take one round from each pair and, using a 1 cm (½ in) fluted round cookie cutter, cut a hole in the centre. Place on the prepared tray.

Bake in the preheated oven 8–10 minutes or until lightly browned on the edges. As the shortbreads will be fragile, allow to cool on the tray before continuing. When cool spread the bases with redcurrant jam and dust the tops with icing sugar. Place the tops on bases.

*Makes 48*

OPPOSITE: *above, Russian Squares; below, Shrewsbury Shortbreads*

# ORANGE TONGUES

*Orange and marzipan combine well in this recipe.*

*120 g (4 oz, ½ cup) butter*
*60 g (2 oz) marzipan (see page 160)*
*60 g (2 oz, ⅓ cup) icing (powdered) sugar*
*150 g (5 oz, 1 ¼ cup) plain (all-purpose) flour*
*zest of 1 orange*
*2 x 60 g (2 oz, large) egg yolks*
*caster (superfine) sugar for decoration*

Preheat oven to 175°C (345°F). Line baking trays (sheets) with baking parchment. Place the butter, marzipan and icing sugar into a mixing bowl and cream together until smooth, light and fluffy. Add the flour, orange zest and egg yolks and fold through quickly but thoroughly. Place the mixture into a piping (pastry) bag fitted with a ½ cm (⅕ in) piping nozzle and pipe 5 cm (2 in) fingers onto the tray. Bake in the preheated oven 8–10 minutes or until lightly golden brown. Cool on the trays. Dip in caster sugar before serving.

*Makes 36*

# PRALINERS

*Not quite a biscuit or cookie but deservedly amongst their ranks. Best eaten the day they are made.*

*210 g (7 ½ oz, 1 cup) caster (superfine) sugar*
*210 g (7 ½ oz, 2 cups) flaked almonds*
*30 g (1 oz, 2 tablespoons) unsalted butter*
*300 g (10 ½ oz) dark (plain or semi-sweet) chocolate, melted (see page 160)*

Line baking trays with baking parchment. Place the sugar in a saucepan over medium heat. Stir continuously, being careful to stir into the corners and over the base where the heat is greatest. Stir until the sugar caramelises, becoming a dark brown liquid. Immediately add the almonds and butter. Stir until well mixed. Quickly place tablespoons of the mixture onto the prepared trays. Using a lightly oiled spoon press them flat. Allow to cool and harden. Spread the base with melted chocolate. Allow to set before serving.

*Makes 18*

# SCOTCH SHORTBREAD

*Shortbread was originally associated with Christmas and New Year's Eve (Hogmanay).*

*480 g (17 oz, 3 ¾ cups) plain (all-purpose) flour*
*300 g (10 ½ oz, 1 ¼ cups) butter*
*150 g (5 oz, ⅔ cup) caster (superfine) sugar*
*caster (superfine) sugar, extra for dusting*

Preheat oven to 175°C (345°F). Line baking trays (sheets) with baking parchment. Place all ingredients into a mixing bowl. Using the fingertips, crumb the butter through the dry ingredients, until mixture resembles fresh breadcrumbs. Scrape the mixture down and form a dough. Knead lightly and shape into two balls of equal size. Flatten the balls by hand onto the prepared tray to form circles 1 cm (⅓ in) thick. Pinch the edges of each disc to give a decorative frilled edge. Using a knife, lightly score the top of both discs. Mark out each into eight wedge-shaped portions, but don't cut to the bottom of the dough. Bake in the preheated oven 20 minutes or until golden brown around the edges. Remove from the oven and sprinkle with extra caster sugar whilst still very hot. Allow to cool on the tray and when cold sprinkle with sugar again.

*Makes 16 wedges, 8 wedges per disk*

OPPOSITE: *above left, Praliners; above right, Scotch Shortbread; below, Orange Tongues*

# SPONGE FINGERS

*Perfect on their own, these fingers can also accompany desserts.*

90 g (3 oz, ⅔ cup) cornflour (US cornstarch)
90 g (3 oz, ⅓ cup) caster (superfine) sugar
5 x 60 g (2 oz, large) egg yolks
75 g (2½ oz, ¼ cup) caster (superfine) sugar, extra
1-2 drops vanilla essence (extract)
3 x 60 g (2 oz, large) eggs whites
75 g (2½ oz, ⅔ cup) plain (all-purpose) flour

Preheat oven to 180°C (350°F). Line baking trays (sheets) with baking parchment. Combine the cornflour and caster sugar. Use half the mixture to lightly dust the lined baking tray. Reserve the remaining cornflour/caster sugar mixture.

Place the egg yolks, extra caster sugar and vanilla into a mixing bowl and whisk to the ribbon stage (see page 159). Place the egg whites into a clean bowl and whisk until they form stiff peaks (see page 159). When both mixtures are ready, fold the flour through the egg yolk mixture and then lightly fold the egg whites through this mixture.

Using a ½ cm (⅕ in) plain piping nozzle attached to a piping (pastry) bag pipe 10 cm (4 in) straight lengths onto the prepared tray. Bake in the preheated oven 10–12 minutes or until the sponge fingers are lightly golden brown. Whilst still hot from the oven, dust the tops of the fingers with the remaining cornflour/caster sugar mixture.

*Makes 36*

# SWISS LINZER

*A scrumptious adaptation of the traditional Austrian Linzer Torte.*

210 g (7½ oz, 1¾ cups) plain (all-purpose) flour
90 g (3 oz, ½ cup) icing (powdered) sugar
120 g (4 oz, ½ cup) unsalted butter
1 x 60 g (2 oz, large) egg
60 g (2 oz, 2 tablespoons) raspberry jam

FILLING
240 g (8½ oz, 1 cup) unsalted butter
150 g (5 oz, ⅔ cup) caster (superfine) sugar
30 g (1 oz, 3 tablespoons) custard powder (cornstarch or English Dessert Powder)
2 x 60 g (2 oz, large) whole eggs
1 x 60 g (2 oz, large) egg yolk
480 g (16½ oz, 2¼ cups) cake crumbs
300 g (10½ oz, 2⅔ cups) ground hazelnuts
150 ml (5 fl oz, ⅔ cup) milk
120 g (4 oz, 1 cup) plain (all-purpose) flour
1½ teaspoons baking powder
1 teaspoon ground cinnamon

Preheat the oven to 175°C (345°F). Grease and line a 30 cm x 25 cm x 3 cm (12 in x 10 in x 1¼ in) baking tray (sheet) with baking parchment. Place the flour and sugar in a bowl. Add the butter and lightly rub into the flour until mixture resembles dry breadcrumbs. Add the egg and mix thoroughly. Turn the dough onto a lightly floured surface and knead lightly. Press the mixture into the prepared tray. Spread with the jam. Spread the filling over the jam-covered base. Bake in the preheated oven 35–40 minutes or until firm to touch. Allow to cool, then cut.

FILLING
Cream the butter, sugar and custard powder until light and fluffy. Add the eggs one by one and the egg yolk and mix well. Add the cake crumbs, hazelnuts, milk, flour, baking powder and cinnamon and mix until well combined.

*Makes 25*

OPPOSITE: *above, Sponge Fingers; below, Swiss Linzer*

# CHEQUERBOARD PIECES

*An elegant treat to serve with coffee.*

### WHITE DOUGH
*210 g (7 ½ oz, 1 ¾ cups) plain (all-purpose) flour*
*90 g (3 oz, ½ cup) icing (powdered) sugar*
*150 g (5 oz, ⅔ cup) unsalted butter*
*2 x 60 g (2 oz, large) egg yolks*

### CHOCOLATE DOUGH
*180 g (6 ½ oz, 1 ½ cups) plain (all-purpose) flour*
*90 g (3 oz, ½ cup) icing (powdered) sugar*
*30 g (1 oz, ¼ cup) cocoa powder*
*150 g (5 oz, ⅔ cup) unsalted butter*
*2 x 60 g (2 oz, large) egg yolks*

*2 x 60 g (2 oz, large) egg whites, lightly beaten*

Line baking trays (sheets) with baking parchment.

To prepare the white dough, sift the flour and icing sugar together and place in a bowl. Rub the butter into the dry ingredients until it resembles coarse breadcrumbs. Add the egg yolks and continue mixing until a dough is formed. To make the chocolate dough, sift the flour, icing sugar and cocoa together and repeat the procedure for the white dough. Wrap each dough in plastic (cling) wrap and refrigerate for 1 hour.

Knead each dough lightly so that it is soft enough to roll. On a lightly floured surface, roll both doughs into a square shape 1 cm (½ in) thick. Cut four 1 cm (½ in) wide strips from the chocolate dough and five 1 cm (½ in) wide strips from the white dough. Knead together any scrap pastry from both doughs into one ball. Roll the scrap pastry out (it should now be a milk chocolate colour) so that it is 2–3 mm (⅛ in) thick, the same length as the white and chocolate strips and at least 16 cm (6 in) wide. Lightly brush the top with egg white.

Place side by side, on top of the milk chocolate pastry, one strip of white pastry, one strip of chocolate pastry and one strip of white pastry. Brush lightly with egg white. Repeat the process on top of this layer, but alternating the colours so that a chocolate strip is placed on top of a white strip and vice versa. Brush this layer with egg white. Create a third layer repeating the process, again alternating the colours. Brush this layer with egg white. Trim any excess pastry from the sides and ends. Lightly brush the sides with egg white. Wrap the milk chocolate pastry around the chequerboard layers. Place in the refrigerator to chill for 1 hour.

Preheat oven to 180°C (350°F). Remove the chequerboard from the refrigerator and cut into 2 mm (⅛ in) thicknesses. Place each piece onto the prepared tray and bake in the preheated oven 8–10 minutes or until lightly golden brown at the edges. Remove from the oven and cool on the tray.

*Makes 24*

**STEP ONE:** *Place side by side on top of the milk chocolate pastry, one strip of white pastry, one strip of chocolate pastry and one strip of white pastry.*

**STEP TWO:** *Repeat the process alternating the strips.*

# TOSCANNER

*A heavenly light almond base crowned with a crisp praline-like topping — a true classic.*

### BASE
*150 g (5 oz, 1 ¼ cup) plain (all-purpose) flour
60 g (2 oz, ⅓ cup) icing (powdered) sugar
90 g (3 oz, ⅓ cup) unsalted butter, softened
1 x 60 g (2 oz, large) egg
1 tablespoon cold water*

### FILLING
*150 g (5 oz, ⅔ cup) unsalted butter
150 g (5 oz, ⅔ cup) caster (superfine) sugar
1 x 60 g (2 oz, large) egg
45 g (1 ½ oz, ⅓ cup) plain (all-purpose) flour
150 g (5 oz, 1 ⅓ cups) ground almonds*

### TOPPING
*55 g (2 oz, ¼ cup) unsalted butter
55 g (2 oz, ¼ cup) caster (superfine) sugar
1 tablespoon clear honey
55 g (2 oz, ½ cup) flaked almonds*

### BASE
Grease and line an 18 cm x 28 cm x 2 cm (7 in x 11 in x ¾ in) baking tray (sheet) with baking parchment. Place the flour and icing sugar in a bowl and very lightly rub in the butter until the mixture resembles coarse breadcrumbs. Add the egg and water and work to a firm dough. Press into the prepared tray with lightly floured hands.

### FILLING
Preheat oven to 180°C (350°F). Place the butter and sugar in a mixing bowl and beat until creamy, light and fluffy. Add the egg and beat for 3 minutes. Beat in the sifted flour and ground almonds. Spread the filling over the pastry-lined tray and bake in the preheated oven 30-35 minutes or until brown and firm to the touch. Cool in the tray.

### TOPPING
Place all the topping ingredients into a saucepan and slowly bring to the boil. Boil for 2 minutes or until the mixture begins to leave the sides of the pan. Using a lightly oiled palette knife, spread the topping mixture over the cooled base. Return to the oven for 10 minutes, then allow to cool thoroughly before cutting into squares.

*Makes 25*

# VANILLA KIPFERLN

*Forming a horseshoe or crescent shape, these pastries symbolise good luck.*

*240 g (8 ½ oz, 1 cup) unsalted butter, softened
120 g (4 oz, ½ cup) caster (superfine) sugar
330 g (11 ½ oz, 2 ¾ cups) plain (all-purpose) flour, sifted
60 g (2 oz, ½ cup) ground hazelnuts
60 g (2 oz, ½ cup) ground almonds
caster (superfine) sugar, extra, for decoration*

Preheat oven to 160°C (320°F). Lightly grease baking trays (sheets).

Place the softened butter and caster sugar into a mixing bowl and mix until well creamed, light and fluffy and pale in colour. Add the sifted flour and ground hazelnuts and almonds and mix until combined.

Take a heaped tablespoon of the mixture and shape into a ball and then roll into a sausage shape, tapering the ends slightly. Bend to form a horseshoe and place onto the prepared tray. Repeat until all the mixture is used. Bake in the preheated oven 10–15 minutes or until lightly golden brown. Remove from the oven and roll each Kipferl carefully in caster sugar. Place on a wire rack until cold. Then roll once more in caster sugar before serving.

*Makes 30*

OPPOSITE: *above, Toscanner; below, Vanilla Kipferln*

# SACHER BARS

*This is an adaptation of the classic Sacher Torte created at the turn of the eighteenth century.*

### BASE
*200 g (7 oz, 1 ¾ cups) plain (all-purpose) flour*
*100 g (3 ½ oz, ½ cup) icing (powdered) sugar*
*120 (4 oz, ½ cup) unsalted butter, cut into small pieces*
*2 x 60 g (2 oz, large) eggs*

### CAKE
*140 g (5 oz, 1 ¼ cups) plain (all-purpose) flour*
*40 g (1 ½ oz, ¼ cup) cocoa powder*
*180 g (6 ½ oz, ¾ cup) unsalted butter*
*100 g (3 ½ oz, ⅓ cup) caster (superfine) sugar*
*6 x 60 g (2 oz, large) egg yolks*
*40 g (1 ½ oz, ⅓ cup) ground hazelnuts*
*6 x 60 g (2 oz, large) egg whites*
*160 g (5 ½ oz, ⅔ cup) caster (superfine) sugar, extra*

### TO DECORATE
*250 g (9 oz, ¾ cup) apricot jam*
*250 ml (9 fl oz, 1 cup) Sacher Bar glaze (see page 156)*
*dark (plain or semi-sweet) chocolate, melted, for piping (see page 160)*

### BASE
Place the flour and icing sugar in a bowl. Add the butter and lightly rub into the flour and icing sugar until the mixture resembles fresh breadcrumbs. Add the eggs and mix thoroughly. Turn the dough onto a lightly floured surface and knead lightly to form a dough. Wrap in plastic (cling) wrap and refrigerate for 30 minutes. Preheat oven to 180°C (360°F). Line a 25 cm x 30 cm x 3 cm (10 in x 12 in x 1 ¼ in) baking tray (sheet) with baking parchment. When rested roll the dough out very thinly on the floured bench. Line the base of the tray with the pastry. Bake in the preheated oven 8–10 minutes or until only just turning brown. Allow to cool in the tray, then remove to a flat surface.

### CAKE
Maintain oven temperature at 180°C (360°F). Grease and line a 25 cm x 30 cm x 3 cm (10 in x 12 in x 1 ¼ in) baking tray (sheet) with baking parchment. Mix the flour and cocoa and sift. Beat the butter and sugar until creamy, light and fluffy. Gradually add the egg yolks and beat well. Gently fold in by hand the sifted flour and cocoa and the hazelnuts. Beat the egg whites until stiff peaks form (see page 159) and gradually add the extra sugar a spoonful at a time. Beat until the sugar is dissolved. Take a quarter of the beaten egg white and gently fold by hand into the mixture. Gently fold in the remaining egg whites. Pour the mixture into the prepared tray and bake in the preheated oven 35–40 minutes or until the top is firm and springs back when lightly touched. Cool in the tray for 5 minutes before turning out onto a wire rack. When cold cut into four layers horizontally.

### TO ASSEMBLE
Spread the apricot jam on the pre-baked base. Place a layer of cake onto the base, one at a time, spreading each lightly with the jam. When all layers have been joined trim the four sides and cut the slab into two separate bars. Boil the remaining apricot jam until thickened and spread evenly over the top and sides of each of the bars. Allow to cool then coat with slightly warm Sacher Bar glaze. Mark into individual serving portions. Decorate each with piped melted chocolate, with the word 'Sacher'.

*Makes 20–24*

**STEP ONE:** *Coat the apricot-glazed cakes with the Sacher Torte Glaze.*

**STEP TWO:** *Decorate each portion with piped melted chocolate.*

# VIENNESE CHERRY SQUARES

*A light cake base topped with the refreshing tang of cherries and covered with a moist butter streusel.*

200 g (7 oz, 1 ¾ cups) plain (all-purpose) flour
2 level teaspoons baking powder
200 g (7 oz, 1 ⅔ cups) cornflour (US cornstarch)
300 g (10 ½ oz, 1 ¼ cup) unsalted butter, softened
300 g (10 ½ oz, 1 ½ cups) caster (superfine) sugar
4 x 60 g (2 oz, large) eggs
100 ml (3 ½ fl oz, ½ cup) milk
400 g (14 oz, 2 ¼ cups) canned sour black cherries (drained)
or 400 g (14 oz, 2 ¼ cups) pitted fresh red cherries

TOPPING
100 g (3 ½ oz, ⅓ cup) caster (superfine) sugar
100 g (3 ½ oz, ⅓ cup) unsalted butter
150 g (5 oz, 1 ¼ cups) plain (all-purpose) flour
60 g (2 oz, ½ cup) ground almonds

Preheat oven to 160°C (320°F). Lightly grease a 25 cm x 30 cm x 3 cm (10 in x 12 in x 1 ¼ in) baking tray (sheet) with butter and line with baking parchment. Mix the flour, baking powder and cornflour together and sift twice. Beat the butter and the sugar until creamy, light and fluffy. Add the eggs one at a time, beating well after each addition. Add the sifted dry ingredients alternately with the milk. Spread the mixture evenly into the prepared pan and top with either the drained black cherries or the fresh pitted cherries. Spread the topping over the cherries. Bake in the preheated oven 30–40 minutes or until cooked. Place the tray on a wire rack to cool. When cold cut into squares.

TOPPING
Mix all the topping ingredients together until the mixture resembles coarse breadcrumbs.

*Makes 25*

# WEINER WAFFLEN

*Viennese delights flavoured with cinnamon and hazelnuts.*

270 g (9 ½ oz, 1 cup) unsalted butter, softened
180 g (6 ½ oz, ¾ cup) caster (superfine) sugar
2 x 60 g (2 oz, large) egg yolks
zest of 1 lemon
15 g (½ oz, 1 tablespoon) ground cinnamon
360 g (12 ½ oz, 3 cups) plain (all-purpose) flour
150 g (5 oz, 1 ⅓ cups) ground hazelnuts
100 g (3 ½ oz, ¼ cup) redcurrant jam
210 g (7 ½ oz) apricot glaze (see page 155)
120 g (4 oz) fondant glaze (see page 155)

Place the butter and sugar in a mixing bowl and cream together until light and fluffy and pale in colour. Add the egg yolks, lemon zest and cinnamon and beat until all are well combined. Add the flour and ground hazelnuts and work mixture to a dough. Remove the dough from the bowl and wrap in plastic (cling) wrap. Refrigerate for 1 hour.

Preheat the oven to 175°C (345°F). Lightly grease an 18 cm x 28 cm x 2 cm (7 in x 11 in x ¾ in) baking tray (sheet). Remove the dough from the refrigerator and knead lightly. Roll half of the dough thinly to fit the base of the tray. Trim the edges to neaten and spread redcurrant jam over the base. Roll out the other half of the pastry and place firmly over the top. Trim to neaten. Bake in the preheated oven 12–15 minutes. Remove from the oven and allow to cool in the baking tray. When cool, brush with apricot glaze and fondant. Cut into squares.

*Makes 24*

OPPOSITE: *above, Weiner Wafflen; below, Viennese Cherry Squares*

# Swiss Cookie Slices

*Flavoured with jam and topped with fondant.*

*405 g (14 ½ oz, 1 ⅔ cups) unsalted butter, cut into small*
*pieces*
*540 g (19 oz, 4 ¼ cups) plain (all-purpose) flour*
*180 g (6 ½ oz, 1 ⅔ cups) ground hazelnuts*
*1 teaspoon mixed spice (see page 161)*
*180 g (6 ½ oz, ¾ cup) caster (superfine) sugar*
*4 x 60 g (2 oz, large) eggs*
*1 tablespoon marmalade*
*210 g (7 ½ oz, ⅔ cup) apricot jam*
*300 g (10 ½ oz) fondant glaze (see page 155)*

Place the butter, flour, ground hazelnuts, mixed
spice and sugar into a bowl and very lightly rub in the
butter until the mixture resembles coarse breadcrumbs. Add the eggs and marmalade and mix to a
firm dough. Wrap the dough in plastic (cling) wrap
and place in the refrigerator for 1 hour. Preheat
oven to 180°C (350°F). Line three 29 cm x 22 cm
(11 ½ in x 8 ½ in) baking trays (sheets) with baking
parchment.

Cut the dough into three equal portions and roll
each portion to fit the prepared trays. Bake in the
preheated oven 10–12 minutes or until lightly golden
brown. Cool on the trays. When cold remove from
tray and peel off baking parchment.

Stack all three pastry sheets on top of each other.
Trim all four sides of the pastry. Cut the trimmed
stack in half along the longest length. Unstack the
pastry sheets and rejoin spreading with apricot jam as
shown. Pour the heated fondant over the top. Using
a palette knife spread the fondant thinly so that it
drizzles down the sides. Allow the fondant to set
before cutting into fine slices with a hot knife.

*Makes 12–18 portions*

**STEP TWO:** *Join all three layers with apricot jam.*

**STEP THREE:** *With the two strips end to end, pour over the heated fondant.*

**STEP FOUR:** *Spread the fondant evenly over the top using a palette knife.*

**STEP ONE:** *Once trimmed stack all three dough sheets on top of each other and cut in half across the longest length.*

# MAI LANDERLI

*Lemon-flavoured German treats.*

*300 g (10 ½ oz, 2 ½ cups) plain (all-purpose) flour, sifted*
*1 teaspoon baking powder*
*150 g (5 oz, ⅔ cup) unsalted butter, softened*
*60 g (2 oz, ¼ cup) caster (superfine) sugar*
*90 g (3 oz, ½ cup) icing (powdered) sugar, sifted*
*5 x 60 g (2 oz) egg yolks*
*zest of 1 lemon*
*1 x 60 g (2 oz, large) egg, lightly beaten*

Place the sifted flour and baking powder, butter, sugar and icing sugar into a mixing bowl and mix together until ingredients resemble coarse bread-crumbs. Add the egg yolks and lemon zest and continue mixing until a dough is formed. Knead the dough lightly, then wrap in plastic (cling) wrap and place in the refrigerator for 1 hour.

Preheat oven to 175°C (345°F). Line baking trays (sheets) with baking parchment. Remove the dough from the refrigerator and again knead lightly. Roll out on a lightly floured surface to 3–4 mm (⅛ in) in thickness. Using a 5 cm (2 in) star-shaped cookie cutter, cut out shapes and place them onto the prepared tray. Brush the tops of the cookies with the lightly beaten egg. Bake in the preheated oven 8–10 minutes or until the cookies begin to turn golden brown. Remove from the oven and allow to cool on the tray.

*Makes 48*

# MONKEY FACES

*An old favourite for cookie stalls and school fêtes. Make sure you have the icing glaze ready as soon as the cookies come out of the oven.*

*450 g (16 oz, 3 ½ cups) plain (all-purpose) flour*
*210 g (7 ½ oz, 1 ¼ cups) icing (powdered) sugar*
*270 g (9 ½ oz, 1 cup) unsalted butter*
*1 x 60 g (2 oz, large) egg*
*redcurrant jam*

### ICING GLAZE
*150 g (5 oz, 1 cup) icing (powdered) sugar*
*2 tablespoons lemon juice*

Sift the flour and icing sugar into a bowl and using your fingers, lightly rub the butter through the dry ingredients until the mixture resembles fresh breadcrumbs. Add the egg and continue mixing to a soft dough. Wrap the dough in plastic (cling) wrap and refrigerate for 1 hour to firm up. Preheat oven to 200°C (400°F). Lightly grease baking trays (sheets). On a lightly floured surface roll the dough out to 3–4 mm (⅛ in) in thickness. With a fluted round cookie cutter, 8 cm (3 in) in diameter, cut out an even number of rounds. Place half the rounds on a tray. These will form the bases of the cookies. Into the remaining rounds cut three small holes using a 1 cm (⅛ in) diameter fluted cookie cutter to make the monkey faces. Place onto the baking tray. Bake both bases and faces in the preheated oven 8–10 minutes or until lightly browned at the edges. Remove from the oven and allow the bases only to cool on the tray. Immediately brush the faces with the icing glaze and allow to cool and set before continuing. Spread the bases with redcurrant jam. Top with the iced faces.

### ICING GLAZE
Sift the icing sugar. Mix in the lemon juice to make a thin icing. If icing is too thick and stiff add extra lemon juice or warm water.

*Makes 12*

OPPOSITE: *above, Mai Landerli; below, Monkey Faces*

# Traditional Favourites

*These recipes have been handed down lovingly through generations of cooks.*

## Anzacs

These Australian favourites are named after the Australian New Zealand Army Corps (ANZAC).

*120 g (4 oz, 1 cup) plain (all-purpose) flour*
*120 g (4 oz, 1 ⅓ cups) rolled oats*
*200 g (7 oz, 1 cup) caster (superfine) sugar*
*90 g (3 oz, 1 cup) desiccated (shredded) coconut*
*150 g (5 oz, ⅔ cup) unsalted butter*
*50 ml (1 ½ fl oz, 3 tablespoons) water*
*60 g (2 oz, 2 tablespoons) golden syrup (light treacle)*
*15 g (½ oz, 2 tablespoons) ground cinnamon*
*1 ½ teaspoons bicarbonate of soda (baking soda)*

Preheat oven to 180°C (350°F). Lightly grease baking trays (sheets). Place the sifted flour, rolled oats, sugar and coconut into a mixing bowl and lightly mix. Place the butter, water, golden syrup and cinnamon in a saucepan and bring to the boil. Add the bicarbonate of soda to the boiling liquid and stir quickly to allow the mixture to foam up. Pour immediately into the dry ingredients and mix well. Take heaped teaspoonfuls of the mixture and roll into balls. Place onto the prepared trays leaving 3–4 cm (1 ½ in) between each Anzac for spreading. Press each ball flat with the back of a spoon. Bake in the preheated oven 10–15 minutes. Remove the tray from the oven. Slide a spatula or palette knife under each Anzac to loosen but leave to cool on the tray. If the Anzacs are not easily loosened return the tray to the oven for a further minute. Store in an airtight container until ready for serving.

*Makes 38–40*

## Kahlua Pecan Squares

Squares rich with maple syrup and Kahlua liqueur.

*210 g (7 ½ oz, 1 ¾ cups) plain (all-purpose) flour*
*90 g (3 oz, ½ cup) icing (powdered) sugar*
*120 g (4 oz, ½ cup) unsalted butter*
*1 x 60 g (2 oz, large) egg*
*210 g (7 ½ oz, 2 cups) pecan nuts, halved*

### Filling
*4 x 60 g (2 oz, large) eggs*
*60 g (2 oz, ⅓ cup) soft (light) brown sugar*
*300 g (10 ½ oz, ¾ cup) golden syrup (light treacle)*
*75 ml (2 ½ fl oz, ⅓ cup) Kahlua liqueur*

Preheat oven to 160°C (320°F). Grease and line a 30 cm x 25 cm x 3 cm (12 in x 10 in x 1 ¼ in) baking tray (sheet) with baking parchment. Place the sifted flour and sugar in a bowl. Add the butter and lightly rub into the flour until mixture resembles dry breadcrumbs. Add the egg and mix thoroughly. Turn the dough onto a lightly floured surface and knead lightly. Press the mixture into the prepared tray. Sprinkle the pecan nuts over the base and pour the filling over the top. Bake in the preheated oven 35–40 minutes or until a knife inserted in the top comes out clean. Cool before cutting into squares.

### Filling
Whisk the eggs with the brown sugar until smooth and lump free. Add the golden syrup and Kahlua to the egg mixture and whisk in well.

*Makes 20*

# BUTTER COOKIES

*Perfect with coffee, these delightful cookies melt in the mouth.*

*240 g (8 ½ oz, 1 cup) unsalted butter*
*60 g (2 oz, ⅓ cup) soft (light) brown sugar*
*240 g (8 ½ oz, 1 ¼ cups) caster (superfine) sugar*
*zest of 1 lemon, grated*
*2 x 60 g (2 oz, large) eggs*
*360 g (12 ½ oz, 3 cups) plain (all-purpose) flour*
*1 tablespoon baking powder*
*1 teaspoon cinnamon*
*150 g (5 oz, 1 ⅓ cups) ground almonds*
*icing (powdered) sugar for dusting*

Preheat oven to 180°C (350°F). Line baking trays (sheets) with baking parchment.

Place the butter, brown sugar and caster sugar and lemon zest into a mixing bowl and cream until light and fluffy. Add the eggs one at a time and mix well between additions. Sift the flour, baking powder and cinnamon and add to the mixture. Add the ground almonds and mix together until all ingredients are well combined.

Place the mixture into a piping (pastry) bag fitted with a 1 cm (⅛ in) plain nozzle. Pipe the mixture into rounds on the prepared tray allowing room for spreading. Bake in the preheated oven 10–12 minutes or until golden brown. Remove and allow to cool slightly on the tray before removing to a wire rack to cool completely. Dust the top of each cookie with icing sugar.

*Makes 48*

# BROWNIES

*Brownies are an American institution.*

*180 g (6 ½ oz, ¾ cup) unsalted butter*
*330 g (11 ½ oz) dark (plain or semi-sweet) chocolate*
*3 x 60 g (2 oz, large) eggs*
*270 g (9 ½ oz, 1 ¼ cups) caster (superfine) sugar*
*90 g (3 oz, ¾ cup) plain (all-purpose) flour*
*360 g (12 ½ oz, 2 ¾ cups) walnuts, chopped*

Preheat oven to 175°C (345°F). Lightly grease and line a 25 cm x 30 cm x 3 cm (10 in x 12 in x 1 ¼ in) baking tray (sheet) with baking parchment.

Melt the butter and chocolate together in a double boiler or bowl placed over a saucepan of boiling water. Place the eggs and the sugar into a mixing bowl and whip until they are light and fluffy and pale in colour. Add the melted chocolate to the whisked egg and sugar mixture and stir well to combine. Add the sifted flour and the chopped walnuts to the chocolate mixture and stir well.

Pour into the prepared tray and smooth out using a spatula or palette knife. Bake in the preheated oven 30–35 minutes or until a thin skewer inserted into the centre comes out clean. Remove from the oven and allow to cool in the tray before cutting into squares and serving.

*Makes 20–25*

OPPOSITE: *left, Butter Cookies; right, Brownies*

# FARMHOUSE GINGER COOKIES

*Some of the best food in the world has been invented in isolated farms and homely kitchens.*

*300 g (10 ½ oz, 2 ½ cups) plain (all-purpose) flour*
*15 g (½ oz, 6 teaspoons) ground ginger*
*½ teaspoon bicarbonate of soda (baking soda)*
*1 tablespoon golden syrup (light treacle)*
*240 g (8 ½ oz, 1 ¼ cups) caster (superfine) sugar*
*120 g (4 oz, ½ cup) butter*
*1 x 60 g (2 oz, large) egg yolk*
*1 tablespoon sour cream*

Preheat oven to 150°C (300°F). Line baking trays (sheets) with baking parchment and lightly dust with cornflour. Place the flour, ginger, bicarbonate of soda, golden syrup, sugar and butter into a mixing bowl. Lightly crumb the mixture until it resembles fresh breadcrumbs. Add the egg yolk and sour cream and continue mixing until a dough is formed. Taking teaspoonfuls of the mixture at a time, roll into balls and place onto the prepared trays, allowing room for spreading. Bake in the preheated oven 10–12 minutes or until cookies become lightly golden brown. Cool on the tray before removing to serve.

*Makes 60 small cookies*

# JAMAICAN BOTERKOEKE SQUARES

*Rich with the flavours of Jamaica — lime and coconut.*

*270 g (9 ½ oz, 1 cup) unsalted butter*
*150 g (5 oz, ⅔ cup) caster (superfine) sugar*
*juice and zest of 1 lime*
*60 ml (2 fl oz, ¼ cup) coconut milk*
*210 g (7 ½ oz, 1 ¾ cups) plain (all-purpose) flour*
*90 g (3 oz, 1 ¾ cups) shredded (flaked) coconut*
*icing (powdered) sugar, for dusting*

Preheat oven to 160°C (320°F). Lightly grease and line a 19 cm x 25 cm x 2 cm (7 ½ in x 10 in x ¾ in) baking tray (sheet) with baking parchment. Place the butter and sugar in a mixing bowl and cream together until light and fluffy. Add the lime juice, zest and coconut milk to the mixture and beat again until all is combined. Sift the flour and add together with the coconut. Mix until all ingredients are incorporated. Spread the mixture evenly into the prepared tray. Bake in the preheated oven 30–35 minutes or until the surface is golden brown in colour. Remove from oven and whilst still hot cut into squares using a sharp knife. Allow to cool for 5 minutes then place squares on a wire rack. Dust with icing sugar before serving.

*Makes 20*

# CHOC CHIP COOKIES

*Perhaps the most popular cookie of them all.*

*120 g (4 oz, ½ cup) unsalted butter*
*120 g (4 oz, ½ cup) sugar*
*90 g (3 oz, ½ cup) soft (light) brown sugar*
*2 x 60 g (2 oz, large) eggs*
*330 g (11 ½ oz, 2 ¾ cups) plain (all-purpose) flour*
*30 g (1 oz, 2 tablespoons) baking powder*
*120 g (4 oz, 1 cup) chocolate chips (drops)*
*60 g (2 oz, ½ cup) walnuts, chopped*

Preheat oven to 175°C (350°F). Grease well baking trays (sheets). Cream together the butter and both sugars until light and creamy. Add the lightly beaten eggs gradually, beating well after each addition. Mix in the sifted flour and baking powder and then add the chocolate chips and chopped nuts. Mix well. Shape small balls of the mixture and place onto the prepared trays. Allow room for spreading. Bake in the preheated oven 10–12 minutes. Remove from the trays carefully and cool on wire racks.

*Makes 48*

OPPOSITE: *above left, Choc Chip Cookies; above right, Jamaican Boterkoeke Squares; below, Farmhouse Ginger Cookies*

# BUTTER STREUSEL FINGERS

*T*errific for parties or morning tea. Prepare the streusel topping first as it can be stored in the refrigerator until needed.

210 g (7 ½ oz, 1 cup) unsalted butter
300 g (10 ½ oz, 2 ½ cups) plain(all-purpose) flour
360 g (12 ½ oz, 1 ¾ cups) caster (superfine) sugar
1 tablespoon baking powder
5 x 60 g (2 oz, large) eggs
100 ml (3 fl oz, ⅓ cup) milk

### STREUSEL TOPPING
100 g (3 ½ oz, ⅓ cup) unsalted butter
100 g (3 ½ oz, ⅓ cup) caster (superfine) sugar
200 g (7 oz, 1 ¾ cups) plain (all-purpose) flour

*icing (powdered) sugar for dusting*

Preheat oven to 180°C (350°F). Grease and line a 25 cm x 30 cm x 3 cm (10 in x 12 in x 1 ¼ in) baking tray (sheet) with baking parchment. Place the butter and flour together in a mixing bowl. Rub through the butter until the mixture resembles breadcrumbs. Add the sugar and baking powder and mix through the butter/flour mixture. Begin adding the eggs very slowly, ensuring that the mixture is well mixed after each addition. When all the eggs have been added continue mixing for a further 2–3 minutes. Scrape the mixture down, making sure that all ingredients are incorporated. Add the milk slowly, again en-suring the mixture is well stirred after each addition. Continue mixing after the milk is incorporated for a further 3 minutes. Spread into the prepared pan. Sprinkle the top with the prepared streusel mixture and then bake in the preheated oven for 35–40 minutes. When baked, cool in the tray and then dust with icing sugar before cutting into finger–sized pieces.

### STREUSEL TOPPING
Place the butter and sugar in a mixing bowl and mix together until they are a smooth combined mass, but not creamed. Add the flour and lightly crumble the mixture together until it resembles large fresh bread-crumbs. Refrigerate until required.

*Makes 30*

# CHOCOLATE DROPS

*T*hese cookies are best served fresh the day they are made as the icing will crystallise when stored.

90 g (3 oz, ⅓ cup) unsalted butter
120 g (4 oz, ½ cup) caster (superfine) sugar
2 x 60 g (2 oz, large) eggs
300 g (10 ½ oz, 2 ½ cups) plain (all-purpose) flour
60 g (2 oz, ½ cup) cocoa powder
30 g (1 oz, 2 tablespoons) baking powder
150 ml (5 fl oz, ⅔ cup) milk
120 g (4 oz, 1 cup) chocolate chips (drops)

### ICING SUGAR GLAZE
150 g (5 oz, 1 cup) icing (powdered) sugar
2 tablespoons water

Preheat oven to 175°C (350°F). Line baking trays (sheets) with baking parchment. Place the butter and sugar into a mixing bowl and cream until light and fluffy. Add the eggs and continue mixing until well combined. Sift the flour, cocoa and baking powder together and then add half to the creamed butter mixture along with half of the milk. Stir until well mixed and then add the remaining milk and dry ingredients. Mix until a smooth batter is formed and then fold through the chocolate chips. Place tablespoonfuls of the mixture onto the prepared tray and bake in the preheated oven 10–15 minutes, or until firm to the touch. Remove from the oven and immediately brush with the icing sugar glaze. Cool on the tray.

### ICING SUGAR GLAZE
Sift icing sugar. Mix with the water. If icing is too stiff add several drops of hot water. If too thin, add a little extra icing sugar.

*Makes 48*

OPPOSITE: *above, Butter Streusel Fingers; below, Chocolate Drops*

# CHERRY RIPE SQUARES

*Topped with cherries and coconut – sure to please.*

*180 g (6 ½ oz, 1 ½ cups) plain (all-purpose) flour*
*90 g (3 oz, ½ cup) icing (powdered) sugar*
*100 g (3 ½ oz, ⅓ cup) unsalted butter, cut into small pieces*
*1 x 60 g (2 oz, large) egg*

### CHERRY MIXTURE
*330 g (11 ½ oz, 1 ½ cups) caster (superfine) sugar*
*330 g (11 ½ oz, 3 ⅔ cups) desiccated (shredded) coconut*
*90 g (3 oz, ⅓ cup) butter, softened*
*3 x 60 g (2 oz, large) eggs, lightly beaten*
*100 g (3 ½ oz, ½ cup) glacé (candied) cherries, chopped*
*60 g (2 oz, ½ cup) dried (dehydrated) milk powder*
*50 ml (1 ½ fl oz, 3 tablespoons) water*

*icing (powdered) sugar, extra for dusting*

Place the flour, icing sugar and butter in a bowl and lightly rub in the butter until the mixture resembles coarse breadcrumbs. Add the egg and rub through the mixture to form a dough. Wrap in plastic (cling) wrap and place in the refrigerator for 1 hour. Preheat oven to 175°C (350°F). Lightly grease and line with baking parchment an 18 cm x 28 cm x 2 cm (7 in x 11 in x ¾ in) baking tray (sheet). Remove the dough from the refrigerator and roll out to cover the base of the prepared tray. Spread the cherry mixture over the base and flatten out using a spatula or the back of a spoon. Bake in the preheated oven 20–25 minutes or until the topping begins to look golden brown all over. Remove from the oven and allow to cool in the tray. When cool cut into squares and dust with icing sugar to serve.

### CHERRY MIXTURE
Place all the ingredients in a mixing bowl and blend together until the butter is well mixed.

*Makes 20*

# CHOCOLATE TUILES

*These cookies are very thin and break easily. It's best to make and eat them the same day.*

*7 x 60 g (2 oz, large) egg whites*
*180 g (6 oz, 1 cup) icing (powdered) sugar*
*60 g (2 oz, ½ cup) plain (all-purpose) flour*
*30 g (1 oz, ¼ cup) cocoa powder*
*75 g (1 ½ oz, ¼ cup) unsalted butter, melted*
*flaked almonds for decoration*

Preheat oven to 180°C (350°F). Lightly grease baking trays (sheets). Whisk the egg whites with the icing sugar until incorporated. Add the flour and cocoa and whisk again. Let the batter rest for 10–15 minutes and then stir in the melted butter.

Place small amounts of the batter on the prepared tray and spread thinly. Bake in the preheated oven 5–8 minutes. It is better to judge when they are cooked by touch rather than by colour. Once baked remove carefully but quickly from the tray using a flat palette knife and roll over a rolling pin or other utensil to give a curved shape until cool and hard. While the cookies are setting, press flaked almonds into them to decorate.

*Makes 18–24*

OPPOSITE: *above, Cherry Ripe Squares; below, Chocolate Tuiles*

# GERMAN HAZELNUT SLICES

*S*erve *in very thin slices as this recipe may taste a
little dry to the uninitiated.*

### BASE
*210 g (7 ½ oz, 1 ¾ cups) plain (all-purpose) flour*
*100 g (3 ½ oz, ½ cup) icing (powdered) sugar*
*130 g (4 ½ oz, ½ cup) unsalted butter, cut into small pieces*
*1 x 60 g (2 oz, large) egg, lightly beaten*
*20 ml (¾ fl oz, 1 tablespoon) water*

### FILLING
*200 g (7 oz, ¾ cup) unsalted butter*
*140 g (5 oz, ⅔ cup) caster (superfine) sugar*
*3 x 60 g (2 oz) eggs*
*200 g (7 oz, 1 ¾ cups) plain (all-purpose) flour*
*210 g (7 ½ oz, 2 cups) ground hazelnuts*

### TO DECORATE
*100 g (3 ½ oz) apricot glaze (see page 155)*
*100 g (3 ½ oz) fondant (see page 155)*

### BASE
Sift the flour. Place the flour and icing sugar in a
bowl. Add the butter and very lightly rub into the
flour and icing sugar until the mixture resembles
fresh breadcrumbs. Add the egg and water and mix
to make a firm dough. Knead very lightly. Wrap in
plastic (cling) wrap and refrigerate for 30 minutes.
Preheat oven to 170°C (340°F). Lightly grease a 25
cm x 30 cm x 3 cm (10 in x 12 in x 1 ¼ in) baking tray
(sheet) and line with baking parchment.

### FILLING
Beat the butter and sugar until creamy, light and
fluffy. Add the eggs one at a time, beating very well
after each addition. Fold in the flour and hazelnuts.

### TO ASSEMBLE
Roll out three quarters of the chilled pastry on a
lightly floured surface. Line the prepared tray with
the pastry and pour in the filling. Spread evenly. Roll
out the remaining pastry thinly and, using a fluted
roller cutter or pizza cutter, cut into 1 cm (½ in)
strips. Arrange the strips in a lattice pattern on top of
the filling. Bake in the preheated oven 35–40
minutes or until cooked. Cool in the pan on a wire
rack. When cool, brush with apricot glaze and allow
to dry before topping with the melted fondant. Cut
into very thin slices.

*Makes 20*

**STEP ONE:** *Cut strips for the lattice pattern using a fluted
roller cutter.*

**STEP TWO:** *Arrange the pastry strips in a lattice pattern on
top of the hazelnut filling.*

**STEP THREE:** *When baked, brush with apricot glaze.*

# DERBY SQUARES

*A buttery cake sprinkled with chocolate chips and pecan nuts.*

210 g (7 ½ oz, 1 ¾ cups) plain (all-purpose) flour
60 g (2 oz, ⅓ cup) icing (powdered) sugar
120 g (4 oz, ½ cup) unsalted butter
2 x 60 g (2 oz, large) egg yolks

### FILLING
3 x 60 g (2 oz, large) eggs
240 g (8 ½ oz, 1 ¼ cups) caster (superfine) sugar
90 g (3 oz, ¾ cup) plain (all-purpose) flour
120 g (4 oz, ½ cup) butter, melted
240 g (8 ½ oz, 2 cups) chocolate chips
90 g (3 oz, ¾ cup) pecan nuts, chopped
1 teaspoon vanilla essence (extract)

icing (powdered) sugar, extra, for dusting

Place flour, icing sugar and butter in a bowl and lightly rub until it resembles coarse breadcrumbs. Add the egg yolks and continue mixing until mixture forms a dough. Wrap in plastic (cling) wrap and refrigerate for 30 minutes. Preheat oven to 160°C (320°F). Line an 18 cm x 28 cm x 2 cm (7 in x 11 in x ¾ in) baking tray (sheet) with baking parchment. Remove the dough from the refrigerator. Press into the tray by hand. Place the filling into the pastry-lined tin and bake in the preheated oven for 40 minutes or until baked. Allow to cool before dusting with icing sugar. Cut into fingers to serve.

### FILLING
Place the eggs and sugar in a mixing bowl and whisk until light, white and fluffy. Fold in the flour and the melted butter. Stir in the chocolate, nuts and vanilla.

*Makes 20*

# DIGESTIVES

*An English favourite, these make a perfect snack lightly spread with butter.*

420 g (15 oz, 3 cups) wholemeal (wholegrain, whole wheat) flour
120 g (4 oz, ¾ cup) oatmeal
1 tablespoon baking powder
120 g (4 oz, ¾ cup) soft (light) brown sugar
180 g (6 ½ oz, ¾ cup) butter
1 tablespoon honey
150 ml (5 fl oz, ⅔ cup) milk

Preheat oven to 180°C (350°F). Line baking trays (sheets) with baking parchment. Place the flour, oatmeal, baking powder and sugar into a mixing bowl. Add the butter and rub through the dry ingredients until the mixture resembles fine bread-crumbs. Add the honey and milk and continue mixing until a dough is formed. If dough is sticky add more flour and if dry add more milk.

Roll out on a lightly floured surface to 4 mm (⅛ in) in thickness. Prick well with a fork and then, using a 8 cm (3 in) plain cookie cutter, cut out rounds. Place directly onto the prepared trays and bake in the preheated oven 15 minutes. Remove and allow to cool on the tray before serving.

*Makes 36*

OPPOSITE: *above, Digestives; below, Derby Squares*

# AFGHANS

Crisp coconut, cereal and chocolate cookies, lavishly dusted with extra chocolate.

210 g (7 ½ oz, 1 cup) unsalted butter
120 g (4 oz, ¾ cup) soft (light) brown sugar
1 x 60 g (2 oz, large) egg
240 g (8 ½ oz, 2 cups) plain (all-purpose) flour
30 g (1 oz, ¼ cup) cocoa powder
2 teaspoons baking powder
pinch of salt
75 g (2 ½ oz, 2 ½ cups) cornflakes
60 g (2 oz, ⅔ cup) desiccated (shredded) coconut
powdered drinking chocolate for dusting

Preheat oven to 180°C (360°F). Line baking trays (sheets) with baking parchment. Place the butter and sugar in a mixing bowl and cream together until light and fluffy. Add the egg and mix until well combined. Sift flour, cocoa powder, baking powder and salt and mix in by hand. Lastly add the cornflakes and coconut, and mix lightly by hand until combined. Place heaped teaspoonfuls of the mixture onto the prepared tray and bake in the preheated oven 10–12 minutes. Allow to cool on the tray before dusting with powdered drinking chocolate and serving.

*Makes 36*

# KISS COOKIES

Unite the lemon-flavoured cakes with raspberry jam to create a mouth-watering kiss.

120 g (4 oz, ½ cup) unsalted butter
120 g (4 oz, ½ cup) caster (superfine) sugar
1 x 60 g (2 oz, large) egg
120 g (4 oz, 1 cup) plain (all-purpose) flour
120 g (4 oz, 1 cup) cornflour (US cornstarch)
1 teaspoon baking powder
1 teaspoon ground cinnamon
zest of 1 lemon
210 g (7 ½ oz, ⅔ cup) raspberry jam
icing (powdered) sugar, for dusting

Preheat oven to 180°C (350°F). Line baking trays (sheets) with baking parchment. Place the butter and sugar in a mixing bowl and cream until light and fluffy. Add the egg and mix until well combined. Add the sifted flour, cornflour, baking powder and cinnamon and stir into the mixture using a wooden spoon. Stir in the lemon zest. Spoon heaped teaspoonfuls of the mixture onto the prepared tray and bake in the preheated oven 10–15 minutes or until lightly golden brown. Cool on a wire rack. When cold join two cookies together with raspberry jam. Dust with icing sugar before serving.

*Makes 12–14*

# SAND COOKIES

A relative of the French sablé.

300 g (10 ½ oz, 1 ¼ cups) unsalted butter
150 g (5 oz) marzipan (see page 160)
150 g (5 oz, 1 cup) icing (powdered) sugar
1 x 60 g (2 oz, large) egg
420 g (15 oz, 3 ⅓ cups) plain (all-purpose) flour
juice and zest of 1 lemon

Preheat oven to 180°C (350°F). Line baking trays (sheets) with baking parchment. Place the butter, marzipan and icing sugar in a mixing bowl and cream together until light and fluffy. Add the egg and mix well. Fold through the sifted flour and the lemon juice and zest. Place the mixture into a piping (pastry) bag fitted with a 1 cm (½ in) star-shaped nozzle and pipe in a swirling motion 6–10cm (2–4 in) lengths onto the prepared trays. Bake in the preheated oven 10–12 minutes or until lightly golden brown and allow to cool on the tray.

*Makes 24*

OPPOSITE: *above, Kiss Cookies; below left, Afghans; below right, Sand Cookies*

# ENGLISH GINGER NUTS

*The traditional Ginger Nut is hard — a real 'nut' to crack!*

*300 g (10 ½ oz, 2 ½ cups) plain (all-purpose) flour*
*1 teaspoon bicarbonate of soda (baking soda)*
*1 teaspoon baking powder*
*15 g (½ oz, 6 teaspoons) ground ginger*
*1 teaspoon mixed spice (see page 161)*
*180 g (6 ½ oz, 1 cup) soft (light) brown sugar*
*60 g (2 oz, ¼ cup) unsalted butter*
*120 g (4 oz, ⅓ cup) golden syrup (light treacle)*
*25 ml (1 fl oz, 2 tablespoons) water*

Sift the flour, bicarbonate of soda, baking powder, ginger and spices into a mixing bowl. Add the brown sugar and stir through well. Crumb the softened butter into the dry ingredients and then add the golden syrup and water. Mix until a dough is formed. Cover the mixture with a damp cloth and leave for 2 hours.

Preheat the oven to 180°C (350°F). Line baking trays (sheets) with baking parchment. Roll the dough out on a lightly floured surface to approximately 2 mm (⅛ in) in thickness. Cut out the Ginger Nuts using a 6 cm (2 ½ in) fluted round cookie cutter. Place on the prepared baking trays and bake in the preheated oven 10–12 minutes. Remove the Ginger Nuts onto a wire rack to cool and serve immediately.

*Makes 24*

# MONTE CARLOS

*As rich as the casino capital of the French Riviera.*

*180 g (6 ½ oz, ¾ cup) unsalted butter*
*150 g (5 oz, ⅔ cup) caster (superfine) sugar*
*1 x 60 g (2 oz, large) egg*
*1 teaspoon vanilla essence (extract)*
*210 g (7 ½ oz, 1 ¾ cups) plain (all-purpose) flour*
*2 teaspoons baking powder*

### FILLING
*90 g (3 oz, ⅓ cup) unsalted butter*
*150 g (5 oz, 1 cup) icing (powdered) sugar*
*1 teaspoon vanilla essence (extract)*
*25 ml (1 fl oz, 2 tablespoons) milk*

*strawberry jam*
*icing (powdered) sugar, extra, for dusting*

Preheat oven to 180°C (350°F). Lightly grease baking trays (sheets). Place the butter and sugar in a mixing bowl and cream until light and fluffy. Add the egg and vanilla. Beat well. Add the sifted flour and baking powder and mix until combined. Roll walnut-sized pieces of the mixture into balls. Place onto the prepared tray. Gently press down with a fork so as to leave an impression. Bake in the preheated oven 10–15 minutes or until golden brown. Remove from the oven and cool on a wire rack. Place a teaspoon of jam and a teaspoon of prepared filling in the centre of half of the Monte Carlos. Top with remaining cookies, press together lightly and then dust with icing sugar.

### FILLING
Cream the butter and sifted icing sugar until light and fluffy. Add the vanilla and the milk. Beat well. Cover with plastic (cling) wrap and store in the refrigerator until required.

*Makes 18*

OPPOSITE: *above, English Ginger Nuts; below, Monte Carlos*

# MARZIPAN ROUT BISCUITS

You *may need to experiment with different brands of marzipan for this recipe until you find the one to give you the best results.*

540 g (19 oz) marzipan (see page 160)
300 g (10 ½ oz, 1 ½ cups) caster (superfine) sugar
3 x 60 g (2 oz, large) egg whites
210 g (7 ½ oz) dark (plain or semi-sweet) chocolate, melted
(see page 160)
glacé cherries for decoration
chopped nuts for decoration

Preheat oven to 200°C (400°F). Line baking trays (sheets) with baking parchment. Place the marzipan and sugar together in a bowl and mix together until they form a solid mass. Slowly add the egg whites until a good piping consistency is formed. (This may take more or less of the egg white depending on the brand of marzipan you use.)

When the mixture is ready (better too stiff than too runny) place into a piping (pastry) bag fitted with a 1 ½ cm (¾ in) star-shaped nozzle or a 1 cm (½ in) plain round nozzle. Pipe the mixture onto the prepared tray in various shapes. Press the halved cherries or nuts into each biscuit or leave plain. Bake in the preheated oven approximately 10–12 minutes. Cool on the tray. Remove the baking parchment. Cover the base of each biscuit with melted chocolate and return to the baking tray. Wrap the tray in plastic (cling) wrap and store in the freezer. Remove 1 hour before eating.

*Makes 36*

# GERMAN HONIG CAKE

A *favourite of German bakers. Enjoy the intense flavours and sweet honey glaze.*

180 g (6 ½ oz, ½ cup) clear honey
60 g (2 oz, 2 tablespoons) golden syrup (light treacle)
30 g (1 oz, 6 teaspoons) unsalted butter
60 g (2 oz, 4 tablespoons) walnut oil
120 g (4 oz, ½ cup) caster (superfine) sugar
30 g (1 oz, 3 tablespoons) ground cinnamon
390 g (14 oz, 3 cups) plain (all-purpose) flour
2 teaspoons baking powder
150 g (5 oz, 1 ⅓ cups) ground almonds
2 x 60 g (2 oz, large) eggs

HONEY GLAZE
2 tablespoons clear honey
1 tablespoon lemon juice
150 g (5 oz, 1 cup) icing (powdered) sugar

Grease and line a 28 cm x 18 cm x 2 cm (11 in x 7 in x ¾ in) baking tray (sheet) with baking parchment. Place the honey, syrup, butter, oil and sugar in a saucepan and bring the mixture to the boil, stirring occasionally to make sure the mixture does not burn. Boil for 2 minutes. Remove and cool. Sift the flour, cinnamon and baking powder into a bowl with the ground almonds and the lightly beaten eggs. Add the cooled butter/honey mixture and work with a wooden spoon until it forms a dough. Remove from the bowl and lightly knead. Press into the prepared tray and smooth. Place into the refrigerator for 2 hours to allow dough to rest. Preheat oven to 180°C (350°F). Remove the dough from the refrigerator and place directly into the preheated oven. Bake for 30–35 minutes or until a skewer inserted in the top comes out clean. Remove and glaze immediately with the honey glaze. Allow to cool before cutting into squares. If the glaze doesn't set after 1 hour, place in the refrigerator to set.

HONEY GLAZE
Place the honey and lemon juice in a bowl and stir until combined. Add the sifted icing sugar and stir until no lumps remain.

*Makes 20–25*

OPPOSITE: *above, Marzipan Rout Biscuits; below, German Honig Cake*

# ROCK CAKES

*T*his English institution is perfect cut in half
and lightly buttered.

*150 g (5 oz, ⅔ cup) unsalted butter*
*180 g (6 ½ oz, ¾ cup) caster (superfine) sugar*
*1 x 60 g (2 oz, large) egg*
*510 g (18 oz, 4 cups) plain (all-purpose) flour*
*30 g (1 oz, 2 tablespoons) baking powder*
*120 g (4 oz, 1 ⅓ cups) desiccated (shredded) coconut*
*250 ml (8 ½ fl oz, 1 cup) milk*
*1 quantity lemon frosting (see page 157)*
*210 g (7 ½ oz, 2 ⅓ cups) desiccated (shredded) coconut,*
*toasted extra*

Preheat oven to 200°C (400°F). Line baking trays
(sheets) with baking parchment.

Place the butter and sugar in a mixing bowl and
cream together until light and fluffy. Add the egg
and continue mixing until well combined. Sift the
flour and baking powder together and add to the
coconut. Add half of the flour, baking powder and
coconut mixture to the butter mix and mix together
with half of the milk, stirring until all ingredients are
combined. Add the remaining dry ingredients and
the milk and combine until the entire mixture is
smooth and well mixed.

Place tablespoonfuls of the mixture onto the
prepared tray, allowing room for spreading. Bake in
the preheated oven 15–20 minutes or until firm to
the touch. Allow to cool on the tray before coating
each Rock Cake with a little frosting and toasted
coconut.

*Makes 18–24*

# PEPPERMINT SQUARES

*A* coconut-flavoured base topped with rich
peppermint filling and crowned with creamy
chocolate.

BASE
*210 g (7 ½ oz, 1 ¾ cups) plain (all-purpose) flour*
*2 teaspoons baking powder*
*120 g (4 oz, ¾ cup) soft (light) brown sugar*
*90 g (3 oz, 1 cup) desiccated (shredded) coconut*
*180 g (6 ½ oz, ¾ cup) unsalted butter, melted*
*½ teaspoon cinnamon*

PEPPERMINT FILLING
*120 g (4 oz) copha (white coconut shortening)*
*360 g (12 ½ oz, 2 cups) icing (powdered) sugar*
*100 ml (3 ½ fl oz, ½ cup) milk*
*1 teaspoon of green-coloured peppermint flavouring*

CHOCOLATE TOPPING
*100 ml (3 ½ fl oz, ½ cup) cream*
*240 g (8 ½ oz) dark (plain or semi-sweet) chocolate, chopped*

Preheat oven to 180°C (360°F). Grease a 28 cm x 19
cm x 2 cm (11 in x 7 ½ in x ¾ in) baking tray (sheet)
and line the base with baking parchment.

BASE
Sift the flour and baking powder and add to the
sugar, coconut, cinnamon and melted butter. Mix all
ingredients until well combined. Press the mixture
into the prepared tray and smooth. Bake in the
preheated oven 20 minutes. Remove from the oven
and allow to cool for 5 minutes before topping with
the peppermint filling.

FILLING
Melt the copha in a small saucepan and then add to
the sifted icing sugar, milk and flavouring. Stir
quickly and continue mixing until all ingredients are
well combined. Pour the mixture onto the warm
base. Spread evenly and then place in the refrigerator to set.

TOPPING
Place the cream in a saucepan and bring to the boil.
Add the chopped chocolate to the hot liquid and stir
until the chocolate is melted and the mixture is
smooth. Allow to cool slightly before pouring over
the set filling. Refrigerate for 2 hours before cutting
into squares.

*Makes 20*

OPPOSITE: *above, Rock Cakes; below, Peppermint Squares*

# MARZIPAN MACAROONS

*The macaroon is one of the oldest styles of cookie. Its origin can be traced back to seventeenth century Italy.*

*100 g (3 ½ oz, ¾ cup) plain (all-purpose) flour*
*50 g (1 ¾ oz, ⅓ cup) icing (powdered) sugar*
*65 g (2 ¼ oz, ¼ cup) unsalted butter, cut into small pieces*
*1 x 60 g (2 oz, large) egg yolk*

TOPPING
*270 g (9 ½ oz) marzipan (see page 160)*
*150 g (5 oz, ⅔ cup) caster (superfine) sugar*
*2 x 60 g (2 oz, large) egg whites*
*apricot jam*

Place the flour and icing sugar in a bowl. Add the butter and lightly rub into the flour and icing sugar until the mixture resembles fresh breadcrumbs. Add the egg yolk and mix thoroughly. Turn the mixture onto a lightly floured surface and knead lightly to form a dough. Wrap in plastic (cling) wrap and chill for 30 minutes.

Preheat oven to 200°C (400°F). Grease baking trays (sheets). Remove the dough from the refrigerator and roll out on a lightly floured surface. Cut 5 cm (2 in) discs of sweet pastry and place onto the prepared tray. Using a small star-shaped nozzle fitted to a piping (pastry) bag, pipe a small ring of marzipan mixture around the edge of the disc. Fill the centre with apricot jam and place in the pre-heated oven 8–10 minutes or until the macaroon is just cooked and the marzipan is just browning around the edges. Store in a completely airtight container, otherwise the marzipan will dry out and go stale.

TOPPING
Place the marzipan and sugar in a bowl and mix together until they form a solid mass. Slowly add the egg whites until a good piping consistency is formed. (This may take more or less of the egg white depending on the brand of marzipan you use.)

*Makes 24–30*

**STEP ONE:** *Pipe a small ring of marzipan around the edge of the disc.*

**STEP TWO:** *Fill the centre with apricot jam.*

# New Orleans Oat Cookies

New Orleans has a rich culinary heritage combining the best of French, Spanish and African cuisines.

120 g (4 oz, 1/2 cup) unsalted butter
240 g (8 1/2 oz, 1 1/2 cups) soft (light) brown sugar
1 tablespoon clear honey
1 x 60 g (2 oz, large) egg
120 g (4 oz, 1 cup) plain (all-purpose) flour
1/2 teaspoon baking powder
150 g (5 oz, 1 cup) oatmeal

Preheat oven to 180°C (350°F). Line baking trays (sheets) with baking parchment. Place the butter and sugar in a mixing bowl with the honey, and cream until light and fluffy. Add the egg and continue mixing until combined. Sift the flour with the baking powder and oatmeal and add to the creamed mixture. Place teaspoonfuls of the mixture onto the prepared trays and bake in the preheated oven 12–15 minutes. Remove and allow to cool for 5 minutes on the trays before removing to wire racks to finish cooling.

*Makes 48*

# Ginger Kisses

Sandwiched together with tangy lemon frosting these cookies make a kiss of perfection.

240 g (8 1/2 oz, 1 cup) unsalted butter
120 g (4 oz, 1/2 cup) caster (superfine) sugar
1 tablespoon golden syrup (light treacle)
1 x 60 g (2 oz, large) egg
330 g (11 1/2 oz, 2 3/4 cups) plain (all-purpose) flour
1 tablespoon baking powder
15 g (1/2 oz, 6 teaspoons) ground ginger
icing (powdered) sugar
1 quantity lemon frosting (see page 157)

Preheat oven to 180°C (350°F). Lightly grease baking trays (sheets). Cream the butter, sugar and golden syrup until light and fluffy. Add the egg and mix well.

Add the sifted flour, baking powder and ginger and work together until a dough is formed. Take small amounts of the dough (the size of a walnut) and roll into a ball. Place onto the prepared baking tray. Using a fork which has been dipped in icing sugar, lightly flatten each ball. Bake in the preheated oven 10–12 minutes. Allow the biscuits to cool on the tray slightly before removing to a wire rack. Join two biscuits together with lemon frosting.

*Makes 20–24*

# Marzipan Almond Horns

A Danish treat, its horseshoe shape symbolises good fortune. You can either roll them in almonds or decorate with royal icing.

540 g (19 oz) marzipan (see page 160)
240 g (8 oz, 1 1/4 cups) caster (superfine) sugar
3 x 60 g (2 oz) egg whites
120 g (4 oz, 1 cup) flaked almonds
210 g (7 1/2 oz) dark (plain or semi-sweet) chocolate, melted (see page 160)

Preheat oven to 200°C (400°F). Line baking trays (sheets) with baking parchment. Place the marzipan and sugar together in a bowl and mix together to form a solid dough. Add all the egg whites slowly. Shape walnut-sized pieces of the mixture into small sausages about 6 cm (2 1/2 in) long. Roll half in flaked almonds. Curve into a horseshoe shape and place onto the prepared tray. Bake in the preheated oven 8–10 minutes and when cool dip bases in chocolate.

*Makes 18–24*

OPPOSITE: *left, New Orleans Oat Cookies; above right, Ginger Kisses; below, Marzipan Almond Horns*

# CHRABELI BREAD

*This Mediterranean recipe can accompany desserts and coffee or is delicious as a snack. The unbaked mixture must dry out 8–10 hours before baking.*

5 x 60 g (2 oz, large) egg whites
240 g (8 oz, 1 ½ cups) icing (powdered) sugar
285 g (9 ½ oz, 2 ¼ cups) plain (all-purpose) flour

Place the egg whites and icing sugar together in a mixing bowl. Using an electric mixer, whip until the mixture is stiff and fluffy. Fold through the flour by hand, stopping as soon as all ingredients are combined. Allow the mixture to sit, covered with a damp cloth, for 1 hour.

Line baking trays (sheets) with baking parchment and lightly dust with cornflour. Knead the dough on a lightly floured surface, keeping the dough and your hands lightly floured to prevent stickiness.

Take heaped tablespoons of the mixture and form into pear shapes. Using scissors or a knife make three cuts down one side of the shape and then place onto the prepared tray. Bend the pieces slightly to open up the three cuts. Allow the Chrabeli Bread to sit uncovered at room temperature for 8–10 hours to dry out and then bake at 200°C (400°F) for 8–10 minutes or until slightly browned.

*Makes 28*

# CUSTARD DREAMS

*It is important not to overmix the butter and dry ingredients in this recipe. Overmixing can cause the custard dreams to lose their melt-in-the-mouth consistency.*

90 g (3 oz, ½ cup) icing (powdered) sugar
210 g (7 ½ oz, 1 cup) unsalted butter
210 g (7 ½ oz, 1 ¾ cups) plain (all-purpose) flour
90 g (3 oz, ⅔ cup) custard powder (cornstarch or English Dessert Powder)
icing (powdered) sugar, extra, for dusting

Preheat oven to 180°C (360°F). Lightly grease baking trays (sheets).

Place the icing sugar, butter and custard powder into a bowl and cream until light and fluffy. Add the sifted flour and stir until all ingredients are well combined. Do not overmix.

Place the mixture into a piping (pastry) bag fitted with a 1 cm (⅛ in) star-shaped nozzle. Pipe small rosettes onto the prepared tray, allowing room for spreading. Bake in the preheated oven 8–12 minutes or until just turning golden brown around the edges. Remove from the oven and immediately place the Custard Dreams on a wire rack to cool. Dust lightly with icing sugar before serving.

*Makes 48*

# MELTING MOMENTS

*The name says it all!*

*240 g (8 ½ oz, 1 cup) unsalted butter, softened*
*90 g (3 oz, ½ cup) icing (powdered) sugar, sifted*
*2 teaspoons vanilla essence (extract)*
*240 g (8 ½, 2 cups) plain (all-purpose) flour, sifted*
*glacé (candied) cherries for decoration*

Preheat oven to 160°C (320°F). Grease baking trays (sheets).

Cream the butter and the icing sugar until almost white, light and creamy. Add the vanilla and mix in well. Add the sifted flour and mix until well combined.

Place the mixture into a piping (pastry) bag, fitted with a 1 cm (½ in) star-shaped nozzle. Pipe small rosettes or stars onto the prepared tray. Decorate each cookie with half a glacé cherry. Bake in the preheated oven 10–15 minutes or until golden brown. Allow to cool on the tray. Remove to a wire rack when cold.

*Makes 36*

# PARIS STICKS

*Soft French shortbread dipped in chocolate.*

*240 g (8 ½ oz, 1 cup) unsalted butter, softened*
*100 g (3 ½ oz, ½ cup) icing (powdered) sugar, sifted*
*1 teaspooon vanilla essence (extract)*
*1 egg white, lightly beaten*
*300 g (10 ½ oz, 2 ½ cups) plain (all-purpose) flour, sifted*
*2 teaspoons lemon juice*
*210 g (7 ½ oz) dark (plain or semi-sweet) chocolate, melted (see page 160)*

Preheat oven to 175°C (345°F). Line baking trays (sheets) with baking parchment.

Place the softened butter, icing sugar and vanilla essence in a mixing bowl and mix until very light and fluffy and pale in colour. Add the slightly beaten egg white and mix in thoroughly to the butter mixture. When combined, add the sifted flour and lemon juice and mix through thoroughly and quickly.

Place the mixture into a piping (pastry) bag, fitted with a 1 cm (½ in) star-shaped piping nozzle. Pipe the mixture onto the prepared trays in 5–6 cm (2 in) lengths, and approximately 2–3 cm (1 in) apart. Bake in the preheated oven 10–15 minutes, or until slightly golden brown. Cool on the tray. When cool, dip 1 cm (½ in) of the shortbread into the melted chocolate. Place back onto the lined tray until set.

*Makes 36*

# ROCKY ROAD

*Relive childhood fantasies with a culinary journey along Rocky Road. If you don't like the flavour of cherries or nuts simply swap them for more marshmallows.*

105 g (3 ½ oz, ¾ cup) plain (all-purpose) flour
15 g (½ oz, 2 tablespoons) cocoa powder
45 g (1 ½ oz, ¼ cup) icing (powdered) sugar
60 g (2 oz, ¼ cup) unsalted butter
1 x 60 g (2 oz, large) egg yolk
1 tablespoon water

### TOPPING
500 g (17 ½ oz) dark (plain or semi-sweet) chocolate, melted
(see page 160)
50 g (1 ¾ oz, 3 tablespoons) copha (white coconut
shortening), melted
200 g (7 oz, 1 cup) marshmallows, cut into small pieces
80 g (2 ¾ oz, ¾ cup) peanuts
60 g (2 oz, ⅓ cup) glacé (candied) cherries, halved

Preheat oven to 175°C (345°F). Grease and line a 19 cm x 28 cm x 2 cm (7 ½ in x 11 in x ¾ in) baking tray (sheet) with baking parchment. Place the flour, cocoa and sugar in a bowl. Add the butter and lightly rub into the flour until mixture resembles dry breadcrumbs. Add the egg and water and mix thoroughly. Turn the dough onto a lightly floured surface and knead lightly. Press the mixture into the prepared tray. Bake in the preheated oven 8–10 minutes. Cool in the tray. Pour the topping onto the cooled base and allow to set at room temperature. Cut into bite-sized pieces and store in the refrigerator.

### TOPPING
Mix the melted chocolate with the melted copha and then pour over the chopped marshmallows, peanuts and cherries. Work quickly, combining the ingredients together.

*Makes 20*

# LEMON, SULTANA AND GINGER BAKED CHEESE DIAMONDS

*Ginger provides added spice to this rich bar.*

105 g (3 ½ oz, ¾ cup) plain (all-purpose) flour
60 g (2 oz, ⅓ cup) icing (powdered) sugar
75 g (2 ½ oz, ¼ cup) unsalted butter, cut into small pieces
1 x 60 g (2 oz, large) egg

### TOPPING
270 ml (9 fl oz, 1 cup) milk
30 g (1 oz, 6 teaspoons) unsalted butter
220 g (7 ½ oz, 1 cup) cream cheese
1 teaspoon ground ginger
juice and zest of 1 lemon
30 g (1 oz, 5 teaspoons) caster (superfine) sugar
125 ml (4 ½ fl oz, ½ cup) milk, extra
50 g (1 ½ oz, ½ cup) custard powder (cornstarch or English
Dessert Powder)
120 g (4 oz, ¾ cup) sultanas (golden raisins)
4 x 60 g (2 oz, large) egg whites
120 g (4 oz, ½ cup) caster (superfine) sugar, extra

2 x 60 g (2 oz, large) egg yolks, beaten

Place the flour, icing sugar and butter into a bowl and crumb the butter through the dry ingredients until the mixture resembles coarse breadcrumbs. Add the egg and mix to a firm dough. Wrap in plastic (cling) wrap and refrigerate for 1 hour. Preheat oven to 180°C (350°F). Grease and line a 25 cm x 30 cm x 3 cm (10 in x 12 in x 1 ¼ in) baking tray (sheet) with baking parchment. Press the dough into the prepared tray. Bake in the preheated oven 8–10 minutes or until light golden brown. Maintain oven temperature. Cool in the tray. Pour the topping onto the cooked base. Brush the top lightly with a beaten egg yolk before baking 25–30 minutes or until firm to the touch. Cool in the tray and then cut into diamond-shaped portions.

### TOPPING
Place the milk, butter, cream cheese, ground ginger, lemon zest and juice and sugar in a saucepan and bring slowly to the boil. Blend the extra milk and custard powder and beat into the mixture as it boils. Cook until thickened, stirring all the time. Remove from the heat. Stir in the sultanas and cool slightly. Beat the egg whites until stiff peaks form (see page 159) and beat in the extra sugar gradually until dissolved. Fold into the custard mixture carefully.

*Makes 20*

OPPOSITE: *above, Rocky Road; below, Lemon, Sultana and Ginger Baked Diamonds*

# RASPBERRY PINWHEELS

*T*ry *experimenting with differently flavoured jam
to the traditional raspberry in this recipe.*

*180 g (6 ½ oz, ¾ cup) unsalted butter
60 g (2 oz, ⅓ cup) icing (powdered) sugar
zest of 1 lemon
1 x 60 g (2 oz, large) egg
210 g (7 ½ oz, 1 ¾ cups) plain (all-purpose) flour
1 teaspoon baking powder
250 g (9 oz, ¾ cup) raspberry jam*

Line baking trays (sheets) with baking parchment.
Place the butter, icing sugar, and lemon zest into a
mixing bowl and cream together until light and
fluffy. Add the egg and mix well. Add to this the
sifted flour and baking powder and continue mixing
slowly until a soft dough is formed. Remove the
mixture from the bowl and wrap in plastic (cling)
wrap and refrigerate for 30–40 minutes.

   Remove from the refrigerator and knead lightly
until the mixture is rollable. Roll on a lightly floured
surface to approximately 2 mm (⅛ in) in thickness,
trying to keep the pastry in a square or oblong shape.
Spread the pastry carefully and thinly with the raspberry jam and then starting from the edge farthest
from you, begin rolling the pastry into a tight Swiss
roll. Refrigerate for 30 minutes.

   Preheat oven to 180°C (350°F).

   Remove the roll from the refrigerator and cut
into 5 mm (¼ in) slices. Place the pinwheels onto the
prepared trays and bake in the preheated oven 10–12
minutes or until golden brown. Cool on the trays.
When cool cut off any jam which may have
caramelised and serve.

*Makes 24*

**STEP ONE:** *Spread the pastry with raspberry jam.*

**STEP TWO:** *Begin rolling the pastry into a tight swiss roll.*

# TOLL HOUSE COOKIES

*This cookie gets its name from the Toll House Restaurant in the United States. Back in the 1930s the owner had the idea of adding chocolate to a basic butter-cookie dough – the chocolate chip cookie was born!*

*180 g (6 ½ oz, ¾ cup) unsalted butter*
*180 g (6 ½ oz, 1 cup) soft (light) brown sugar*
*180 g (6 ½ oz, ¾ cup) caster (superfine) sugar*
*2 x 60 g (2 oz, large) eggs*
*300 g (10 ½ oz, 2 ½ cups) plain (all-purpose) flour*
*1 teaspoon baking powder*
*300 g (10 ½ oz, 1 ¼ cups) dark (plain or semi-sweet) chocolate chips (drops)*
*210 g (7 ½ oz, 1 cup) milk chocolate chips (drops)*

Preheat oven to 180°C (350°F). Line baking trays (sheets) with baking parchment.

Place the butter and both sugars in a mixing bowl and whip until light and fluffy. Add the eggs one at a time and mix well between additions. Sift the flour and the baking powder and add to the butter mixture with both amounts of chocolate chips. Stir until well combined.

Take tablespoonfuls of the mixture and place onto the prepared trays, allowing room (twice the size of the unbaked cookie) for spreading. Bake in the preheated oven 15–20 minutes or until cookies are golden brown and firm to touch. Remove and cool on the tray.

*Makes 24*

# VIENNESE COOKIES

*One of the finest cookies created – soft and melting.*

*240 g (8 ½ oz, 1 cup) unsalted butter, softened*
*100 g (3 ½ oz, ½ cup) icing (powdered) sugar, sifted*
*2 teaspoons vanilla essence (extract)*
*1 x 60 g (2 oz, large) egg, lightly beaten*
*300 g (10 ½ oz, 2 ½ cups) plain (all-purpose) flour, sifted*
*210 g (7 ½ oz) dark (plain or semi-sweet) chocolate, melted (see page 160)*
*icing (powdered) sugar, extra, for dusting*

Preheat oven to 175°C (345°F). Line baking trays (sheets) with baking parchment.

Place the softened butter, icing sugar and vanilla essence into a mixing bowl and mix until very light and fluffy and pale in colour. Add the slightly beaten egg and mix in thoroughly to the butter mixture. When combined, add the sifted flour and mix thoroughly and quickly.

Place the mixture into a piping (pastry) bag, fitted with a 1 cm (½ in) star-shaped nozzle. Pipe the mixture onto the prepared trays in 5–6 cm (2 ½ in) lengths, and approximately 2–3 cm (1 in) apart. Bake in the preheated oven 10–12 minutes, or until lightly golden brown. Allow to cool on the tray. When cool, dip the cookies carefully into the melted chocolate so that only half of the length of the cookie is covered. Place back onto the lined tray and when all cookies have been dipped, place the tray into the refrigerator for several minutes until the chocolate sets. Dust the uncovered half of the cookie with icing sugar.

*Makes 56*

OPPOSITE: *above, Viennese Cookies; below, Toll House Cookies*

# BATH BISCUITS

*An English favourite, crisp and sweet with a hint of spice.*

300 g (10 ½ oz, 2 ½ cups) plain (all-purpose) flour
150 g (5 oz, 1 cup) icing (powdered) sugar
1 teaspoon ground cinnamon
150 g (5 oz, ⅔ cup) unsalted butter
1 x 60 g (2 oz, large) egg
1 tablespoon water
120 g (4 oz, ¾ cup) currants
1 quantity egg wash (see page 156)
caster (superfine) sugar for decoration

Line baking trays (sheets) with baking parchment. Place the flour, icing sugar, cinnamon and butter into a bowl and lightly crumb the butter through the other ingredients until the mixture resembles coarse breadcrumbs. Add the lightly beaten egg and the water and work the mixture to a dough. Finally add the currants and knead through the dough lightly. Wrap in plastic (cling) wrap and place in the refrigerator for 30 minutes.

Preheat the oven to 180°C (350°F). Remove the dough from the refrigerator and knead until ready to roll. Roll on a lightly floured surface to 4 mm (⅛ in) in thickness. Cut small discs using a 10 cm (4 in) fluted round cookie cutter and place directly onto the prepared trays. Lightly egg wash each disc and sprinkle lightly with caster sugar. Bake in the preheated oven 8–12 minutes or until lightly golden brown. Remove and cool on trays before serving.

*Makes 18–24*

# BAKED CHOCOLATE CHEESECAKE SQUARES

*To ensure success, don't open the oven after the heat is reduced, and store the cheesecake in the refrigerator as long as possible before cutting.*

180 g (6 ½ oz, 1 ⅔ cup) biscuit (cookie) crumbs
30 g (1 oz, 5 teaspoons) caster (superfine) sugar
30 g (1 oz, ¼ cup) cocoa powder
60 g (2 oz, ¼ cup) unsalted butter, melted

### FILLING
660 g (1 lb 7 oz) cream cheese
240 g (8 ½ oz, 1 ¼ cups) caster (superfine) sugar
180 g (6 ½ oz) dark (plain or semi-sweet) chocolate, melted (see page 160)
60 g (2 oz) white chocolate, melted
2 x 60 g (2 oz, large) eggs
30 g (1 oz, 4 tablespoons) thickened (double or heavy) cream
90 g (3 oz, ⅓ cup) sour cream
75 g (2 ½ oz, ⅔ cup) instant coffee granules dissolved in 1 tablespoon water

Preheat oven to 160°C (320°F). Lightly grease and line a 25 cm x 30 cm x 3 cm (10 in x 12 in x 1 ¼ in) baking tray (sheet), with baking parchment. Place the biscuit crumbs, sugar and cocoa powder into a mixing bowl. Add the melted butter and stir until all ingredients are well combined. Press the mixture into the prepared tray and smooth with the back of a spoon. Pour the filling over the base. Bake in the preheated oven 40 minutes, then turn the oven off and leave the cheesecake in the oven for a further 40 minutes in the dying heat. Remove from oven and place in the refrigerator for 24 hours before cutting into squares to serve.

### FILLING
Place the cream cheese into a mixing bowl with the sugar and whip together until smooth and lump free. Add the melted dark and white chocolate and continue whipping so that no lumps of chocolate form. Add the eggs one at a time and mix well between additions. Scrape down the sides of the bowl to make sure all mixture is incorporated. Add the double cream, sour cream and coffee and mix well until all is combined.

*Makes 20*

OPPOSITE: *above, Baked Chocolate Cheesecake Squares; below, Bath Biscuits*

# RICHLY REWARDING

*Indulge yourself with these rich treats.*

## SWEET POPPY SQUARES

Poppy seeds and lemon cream cheese frosting create a tangy, rich bar.

*210 g (7 ½ oz, 1 cup) unsalted butter*
*120 g (4 oz, ½ cup) caster (superfine) sugar*
*5 x 60 g (2 oz, large) egg yolks*
*240 g (8 ½ oz, 1 ½ cups) poppy seeds*
*1 teaspoon ground ginger*
*120 g (4 oz, 1 cup) plain (all-purpose) flour*
*5 x 60 g (2 oz, large) egg whites*
*120 g (4 oz, ½ cup) caster (superfine) sugar, extra*
*1 quantity lemon cream cheese frosting (see page 157)*

Preheat oven to 180°C (350°F). Grease and line a 25 cm x 30 cm x 3 cm (10 in x 12 in x 1 ¼ in) baking tray (sheet) with baking parchment. Place the butter and sugar in a mixing bowl and cream until light and fluffy. Add the egg yolks slowly and mix until well combined. Add the poppy seeds, ground ginger and flour and mix well. Whisk the egg whites until stiff peaks form (see page 159) then slowly add the extra sugar until all is dissolved. Carefully fold the whisked egg whites through the poppy seed mixture. Spread the mixture into the prepared tray and bake in the preheated oven 20–25 minutes or until the top springs back when lightly touched. Remove and allow to cool before spreading the top with lemon cream cheese frosting. Cut into squares.

*Makes 30–35*

## FEATHER LIGHT ALMOND DELIGHT

Whipped egg whites provide the soft, light texture in this treat.

*5 x 60 g (2 oz, large) egg yolks*
*150 g (5 ½ oz, ⅔ cup) caster (superfine) sugar*
*330 g (11 ½ oz, 3 cups) ground almonds*
*180 g (6 ½ oz, ¾ cup) unsalted butter, melted and cooled*
*4 x 60 g (2 oz, large) egg whites*
*120 g (4 oz, ½ cup) caster (superfine) sugar, extra*
*icing (powdered) sugar for dusting*

Preheat oven to 180°C (350°F). Grease and line a 25 cm x 30 cm x 3 cm (10 in x 12 in x 1 ¼ in) baking tray (sheet) with baking parchment. In a mixing bowl beat the egg yolks and sugar until thick and pale and the mixture forms a ribbon (see page 159). Gently fold in the ground almonds and the melted butter. Beat the egg whites until stiff peaks form (see page 159). Gradually beat in the extra sugar, a spoonful at a time until the sugar is completely dissolved. Scoop out a spoonful of the mixture and mix in by hand into the beaten egg yolks. Gently fold in the remainder of the beaten egg whites. Pour the mixture into the prepared tray and bake in the preheated oven 25–30 minutes or until the top is springy to the touch and the cake has shrunk from the sides of the tray. Allow to cool in the tray. Dust with icing sugar and cut into finger-sized portions.

*Makes 25–30*

OPPOSITE: *above, Sweet Poppy Squares; below, Feather Light Almond Delight*

# CITRUS FINGER DELIGHTS

*The word 'luscious' was invented for this slice.*

*120 g (4 oz, ½ cup) unsalted butter*
*90 g (3 oz, ½ cup) icing (powdered) sugar*
*150 g (5 oz, 1 ¼ cups) plain (all-purpose) flour*

### TOPPING
*2 x 60 g (2 oz, large) eggs*
*zest and juice of 1 lemon*
*zest and juice of 1 orange*
*30 g (1 oz, ¼ cup) plain (all-purpose) flour*
*240 g (8 ½ oz, 1 ¼ cups) caster (superfine) sugar*

*icing (powdered) sugar, extra, for dusting*

Preheat oven to 160°C (320°F). Grease and line an 18 cm x 28 cm x 2 cm (7 in x 11 in x ¾ in) baking tray (sheet) with baking parchment. Place the butter, icing sugar and flour into a mixing bowl and mix together until combined and smooth and soft in texture. Press the mixture evenly and smoothly into the base of the prepared tray and bake in the pre-heated oven 15 minutes or until just beginning to brown. Remove and allow to cool in the tray. Maintain oven temperature. Pour the topping over the prepared base and return the tray to the oven for a further 20 minutes. Remove and immediately dust with sifted icing sugar. Allow to cool in the tray for 2 hours before cutting into fingers.

### TOPPING
Lightly whisk the eggs. Add the lemon and orange zest and juice and whisk to combine. Place the flour and sugar into a separate bowl and whilst whisking add the egg mixture. Whisk until smooth.

*Makes 20*

# MISSISSIPPI MUD SQUARES

*A classic of American confectionery.*

*360 g (12 ½ oz, 3 cups) plain (all-purpose) flour*
*2 ½ teaspoons baking powder*
*4 level teaspoons bicarbonate of soda (baking soda)*
*60 g (2 oz, ½ cup) cocoa powder*
*120 g (4 oz, ½ cup) unsalted butter*

*360 g (12 ½ oz, 2 cups) soft (light) brown sugar*
*2 x 60 g (2 oz, large) eggs*
*150 g (5 oz) dark (plain or semi-sweet) chocolate, melted (see page 160)*
*230 ml (8 fl oz, 1 cup) milk*
*1 teaspoon vanilla essence (extract)*
*1 quantity chocolate frosting (see page 158)*

Preheat oven to 180°C (350°F). Grease and line a 25 cm x 30 cm x 3 cm (10 in x 12 in x 1 ¼ in) baking tray (sheet) with baking parchment. Sift the flour, baking powder, bicarbonate of soda and cocoa powder twice. Beat the butter and sugar until they are well combined in a soft paste. Add the eggs one at a time, beating well after each addition. Add the melted chocolate to the butter mixture and beat in well. Mix in by hand the sifted dry ingredients alternately with the milk and vanilla essence. Pour into the prepared tray and bake in the preheated oven 35–40 minutes or until firm to the touch. Cool in the tray. When cold cover the top with the chocolate frosting. Cut into small squares to serve.

*Makes 36*

# FUDGE BROWNIES

*Every chocoholic's dream come true.*

*150 g (5 oz, ⅔ cup) unsalted butter*
*180 g (6 ½ oz) dark (plain or semi-sweet) chocolate*
*210 g (7 ½ oz, 1 ⅓ cup) soft (light) brown sugar, firmly packed*
*60 g (2 oz, 2 tablespoons) honey*
*2 x 60 g (2 oz, large) eggs*
*240 g (8 ½ oz, 2 cups) plain (all-purpose) flour*
*120 g (4 oz, 1 cup) walnuts, chopped*
*90 g (3 oz, ¾ cup) almonds, chopped*

Preheat oven to 175°C (345°F). Grease and line a 25 cm x 30 cm x 3 cm (10 in x 12 in x 1 ¼ in) baking tray (sheet) with baking parchment. Melt the butter and chocolate in a bowl over a saucepan of boiling water (double boiler). Remove from the heat and stir in the sugar and honey. Stir in the eggs one at a time, then the sifted flour and chopped nuts. Pour the mixture into the prepared tray and bake in the preheated oven 30 minutes or until firm to the touch. Cool in the tray before cutting to serve.

*Makes 20–24*

OPPOSITE: *above, Mississippi Mud Squares; centre, Fudge Brownies; below, Citrus Finger Delights*

# CHOCOLATE SUPREME

*The cocoa bean from which chocolate is made is known botanically as* Theobroma cacao — *'food of the gods'. This recipe will help you see why!*

*105 g (3 ¹/₂ oz, ³/₄ cup) plain (all-purpose) flour*
*45 g (1 ¹/₂ oz, 3 tablespoons) icing (powdered) sugar*
*60 g (2 oz, ¹/₄ cup) unsalted butter*
*1 x 60 g (2 oz, large) egg yolk*
*400 ml (14 fl oz, 1 ³/₄ cup) sweetened condensed milk*
*60 g (2 oz, ²/₃ cup) desiccated (shredded) coconut*
*60 g (2 oz, ¹/₂ cup) macadamia (Queensland) nuts, chopped*
*210 g (7 ¹/₂ oz) dark (plain or semi-sweet) chocolate chips (drops)*

Preheat oven to 160°C (320°F). Grease and line a 19 cm x 28 cm x 2 cm (7 ¹/₂ in x 11 in x ³/₄ in) baking tray (sheet) with baking parchment.

Place the flour and sugar in a bowl. Add the butter and lightly rub into the flour until mixture resembles dry breadcrumbs. Add the egg yolk and mix thoroughly. Turn the dough onto a lightly floured surface and knead lightly. Press the mixture into the prepared tray. Bake in the preheated oven 8–10 minutes or until golden brown.

Reduce oven temperature to 145°C (290°F). Pour half of the sweetened condensed milk over the baked base. Sprinkle with the coconut, macadamias and chocolate chips and then pour the other half of the condensed milk over the top. Place into the cooler oven and bake for 40 minutes. Remove and allow to cool for 2 hours before cutting into small fingers.

*Makes 24*

# COCONUT MACAROONS

*Rich and very moist. You will need a sugar (candy) thermometer for this recipe.*

*300 g (10 ¹/₂ oz, 3 ¹/₂ cups) desiccated (shredded) coconut*
*450 g (16 oz, 2 ¹/₄ cups) caster (superfine) sugar*
*6 x 60 g (2 oz, large) egg whites*
*juice of 1 lemon*
*dark (plain or semi-sweet) chocolate, melted (see page 160)*

Preheat oven to 180°C (350°F). Line baking trays (sheets) with baking parchment.

Place the coconut and sugar in a large saucepan and stir with a wooden spoon slightly to mix. Add the egg whites and lemon juice and stir the mixture to a moist paste. Place the saucepan over a low heat and stir continuously until the mixture reaches 40°C (104°F). Remove the pan from the heat and continue mixing until the mixture cools.

Place into a piping (pastry) bag fitted with a 1 ¹/₂ cm (³/₄ in) star-shaped piping nozzle. Pipe into rosette shapes onto the prepared tray leaving 1–2 cm (1 in) between each. Bake in the preheated oven 10–15 minutes or until just beyond golden brown. Cool on the tray. Dip the base of each macaroon into the melted chocolate. Allow the chocolate to set before serving.

*Makes 36*

OPPOSITE: *above, Coconut Macaroons; below, Chocolate Supreme*

# HAZELNUT SUPREMES

*Perfect with coffee at the end of a meal.*

*190 g (6 ½ oz, 1 ½ cups) plain (all-purpose) flour*
*100 g (3 ½ oz, ½ cup) icing (powdered) sugar*
*150 g (5 oz, ⅔ cup) unsalted butter, cut into small pieces*
*1 x 60 g (2 oz, large) egg*
*15 ml (½ fl oz, 1 tablespoon) water*

### FILLING
*240 g (8 ½ oz, 2 ¼ cups) ground hazelnuts*
*390 g (14 oz, 2 cups) caster (superfine) sugar*
*7 x 60 g (2 oz) egg whites*

Place the flour and icing sugar in a bowl. Add the butter and very lightly rub into the flour until the mixture resembles fresh breadcrumbs. Add the egg and sufficient water to make a firm dough. Knead very lightly and wrap in plastic (cling) wrap. Refrigerate for 1 hour. Preheat oven to 175°C (345°F). Grease and line a 19 cm x 28 cm x 2 cm (7 ½ in x 11 in x ¾ in) baking tray (sheet) with baking parchment. Remove dough from the refrigerator. Lightly knead so that it is soft enough to roll. Roll out on a lightly floured surface to line the base of the prepared baking tray. Bake in the preheated oven 12 minutes, to precook lightly. Remove and allow to cool in the tray. Maintain oven temperature. Pour the filling onto the pastry base and spread evenly. Bake 15–20 minutes or until golden brown. Remove from the oven and allow to cool in the tray. Cut into squares. Store in an airtight container.

### HAZELNUT FILLING
Place the ground hazelnuts, sugar and egg whites into a large saucepan and stir together using a wooden spoon until the mixture is combined. Place over medium heat and slowly bring to the boil. Stir constantly, making sure that none of the mixture burns. Once the mixture is boiling stir vigorously until it begins to boil clear of the sides of the saucepan. Remove from heat and allow to cool slightly.

*Makes 20–24*

**STEP ONE:** *Stir the filling constantly, making sure none of the mix catches on the base.*

**STEP TWO:** *Once the mixture is boiling stir vigorously until the mixture begins to boil clear of the sides of the saucepan.*

**STEP THREE:** *Pour the filling onto the pastry base and spread evenly.*

# ALMOND SWIRLS

A *crisp base topped with smooth and creamy chocolate, laced with Grand Marnier.*

300 g (10 ½ oz, 2 ½ cups) plain (all-purpose) flour
150 g (5 oz, 1 cup) icing (powdered) sugar
1 teaspoon ground cinnamon
150 g (5 oz, ⅔ cup) unsalted butter
1 x 60 g (2 oz, large) egg
1 tablespoon water

### GANACHE TOPPING
200 ml (7 fl oz, 1 cup) thickened (double or heavy) cream
75 ml (2 ½ fl oz, ⅓ cup) Grand Marnier liqueur
500 g (17 ½ oz) dark (plain or semi-sweet) chocolate, melted (see page 160)

240 g (8 ½ oz, 1 ½ cups) roasted whole blanched (skinned) almonds, for decoration
250 g (9 oz) dark (plain or semi-sweet) chocolate, melted, extra

Line baking trays (sheets) with baking parchment. Place the flour, icing sugar, cinnamon and butter into a bowl and lightly crumb the butter through the other ingredients until the mixture resembles coarse breadcrumbs. Add the lightly beaten egg and the water and work to a dough. Wrap in plastic (cling) wrap and place in the refrigerator for 30 minutes. Preheat oven to 180°C (350°F). Remove the dough and knead until ready to roll. Roll on a lightly floured surface as thinly as possible. Cut out small discs using a 5 cm (2 in) diameter fluted round cookie cutter. Place the discs directly onto the prepared trays. Bake in the preheated oven 8–12 minutes or until lightly golden brown. Remove and cool on a wire rack. Pipe a neat rosette of ganache onto the smooth (bottom) side of each disc. Place a roasted whole almond in the centre of each ganache rosette. Lift the swirl by the almond and dip the base into the melted chocolate. Place on to a tray lined with baking parchment and refrigerate until set.

### GANACHE TOPPING
Place the cream and Grand Marnier in a saucepan and bring to the boil. As soon as the mixture boils remove from the heat and add the melted chocolate. Stir until a thick, smooth consistency is reached. Allow to cool and then place in the refrigerator, stirring every five minutes until the mixture thickens to piping consistency.

*Makes 48*

# GOLDEN PECAN COOKIES

P*ecan nuts and chocolate have always been a devastating combination — never more so than in this rich recipe.*

120 g (4 oz, ½ cup) unsalted butter
150 g (5 oz, 1 cup) soft (light) brown sugar
2 teaspoons golden syrup (light treacle)
1 x 60 g (2 oz, large) egg yolk
15 ml (½ fl oz, 1 tablespoon) milk
180 g (6 ½ oz, 1 ½ cups) plain (all-purpose) flour
½ teaspoon baking powder
90 g (3 oz, ¾ cup) pecan nuts, chopped
210 g (7 ½ oz) dark (plain or semi-sweet) chocolate, melted (see page 160)

Place the butter, brown sugar and golden syrup in a mixing bowl and mix until well combined. Then cream until light and fluffy. Add the egg yolk and milk and beat until well incorporated. Add the sifted flour, baking powder and pecan nuts, mixing until all ingredients are combined. Divide the dough into five equal portions and roll them into sausage shapes. Wrap each in plastic (cling) wrap and refrigerate for 1 hour.

Preheat oven to 175°C (345°F). Line baking trays (sheets) with baking parchment. Remove the dough from the refrigerator and discard plastic (cling) wrap. Cut into 5 mm (⅛ in) slices. Place each slice onto the prepared tray. Bake in the preheated oven 8–10 minutes or until just turning golden brown. Remove from the tray to a wire rack immediately. When cool drizzle melted chocolate over each cookie.

*Makes 29*

OPPOSITE: *above, Almond Swirls; below, Golden Pecan Slices*

# CINNAMON ALMOND FINGERS

*W*onderfully moist, cinnamon-flavoured fingers.

210 g (7 ¹/₂ oz, 1 ³/₄ cup) plain (all-purpose) flour
60 g (2 oz, ¹/₃ cup) icing (powdered) sugar
120 g (4 oz, ¹/₂ cup) unsalted butter

### FILLING
3 x 60 g (2 oz, large) eggs
180 g (6 ¹/₂ oz, ³/₄ cup) caster (superfine) sugar
150 ml (5 fl oz, ²/₃ cup) cream (single, light)
150 ml (5 fl oz, ²/₃ cup) milk
30 g (1 oz, 3 tablespoons) ground cinnamon
210 g (7 ¹/₂ oz, 2 cups) ground almonds
15 g (¹/₂ oz, 1 tablespoon) baking powder

### VANILLA FROSTING
500 g (17 ¹/₂ oz, 3 cups) icing (powdered) sugar, sifted
40 g (1 ¹/₂ oz, 1 tablespoon) glucose (corn) syrup
60 g (2 oz, ¹/₄ cup) unsalted butter
60 ml (2 fl oz, ¹/₄ cup) water
1 teaspoon vanilla essence (extract)
cinnamon, extra, for dusting

Place the flour, icing sugar and butter in a bowl and lightly rub with fingers until the mixture resembles fresh breadcrumbs. Continue mixing to a soft but solid dough. Wrap in plastic (cling) wrap and place in the refrigerator for 30 minutes. Preheat oven to 160°C (320°F). Lightly grease a 28 cm x 18 cm x 3 cm (11 in x 7 in x 1 ¼ in) baking tray (sheet). Roll the dough out on a lightly floured surface to cover the base and sides of the tray. Pour the filling over the prepared base. Bake in the preheated oven 35–40 minutes or until judged cooked. Allow to cool in the tray. Top with the frosting and dust with cinnamon. Cut into fingers.

### FILLING
Place the eggs in a bowl and whisk lightly. Add the sugar, cream and milk and again whisk lightly to incorporate all ingredients. Add the cinnamon, ground almonds and baking powder and stir well.

### VANILLA FROSTING
Place the butter, icing sugar and glucose in a bowl and blend slowly. Slowly add the water and vanilla a little at a time and mix thoroughly after each addition. Beat for 15 minutes at top speed until the frosting is white, light and fluffy.

*Makes 20*

# CHOCOLATE HEAVEN

*P*ecan nuts add a special touch to this delicious relative of the brownie.

90 g (3 oz, ¹/₃ cup) unsalted butter
240 g (8 ¹/₂ oz, 1 ¹/₄ cups) caster (superfine) sugar
105 g (3 ¹/₂ oz, ³/₄ cup) plain (all-purpose) flour, sifted
60 g (2 oz, ¹/₂ cup) pecan nuts, finely chopped
2 x 60 g (2 oz, large) eggs
30 g (1 oz, ¹/₄ cup) cocoa powder, sifted
icing (powdered) sugar for dusting

Preheat oven to 160°C (320°F). Grease and line an 18 cm x 28 cm x 2 cm (7 in x 11 in x ¾ in) baking tray (sheet) with baking parchment.

Place all ingredients except the icing sugar in a mixing bowl and beat until combined. Continue mixing for a further 5 minutes. Allow the mixture to rest briefly before pouring into the prepared tray.

Bake in the preheated oven 20 minutes or until firm. Remove from oven and dust with icing sugar. Allow to cool in the tray for 1 hour before cutting into fingers.

*Makes 20*

# FESTIVE TREATS

*Help celebrate any festive occasion with
these traditional recipes.*

## GINGERBREAD SQUARES

Spicy squares topped with lemon frosting.

*120 g (4 oz, ½ cup) unsalted butter*
*240 g (8 ½ oz, 1 ¼ cups) caster (superfine) sugar*
*360 g (12 ½ oz, 1 cup) golden syrup (light treacle)*
*2 x 60 g (2 oz, large) eggs*
*15 g (½ oz, 1 tablespoon) bicarbonate of soda (baking soda),
dissolved in a tablespoon boiling water*
*15 g (½ oz, 6 teaspoons) ground ginger*
*1 teaspoon mixed spice (see page 161)*
*330 g (11 ½ oz, 2 ¾ cups) plain (all-purpose) flour*
*250 ml (9 fl oz, 1 cup) milk*
*1 quantity lemon cream cheese frosting (see page 157)*
*ground cinnamon for dusting*

Preheat oven to 180°C (350°F). Grease and line a 25 cm x 30 cm x 3 cm (10 in x 12 in x 1 ¼ in) baking tray (sheet) with baking parchment. Place the butter and sugar in a mixing bowl and cream until light and fluffy. Scrape down the bowl and add the golden syrup and continue creaming the mixture until completely combined. Add the eggs one at a time, mixing well after each addition. Add the bicarbonate of soda mixed with the boiling water, along with the spices, ginger, half the flour and half the milk. Mix well before adding the remaining flour and milk. Continue mixing until smooth. Pour the mixture into the prepared tray and bake in the preheated oven 45–50 minutes or until a skewer inserted in the centre comes out clean. Allow to cool in the tray before icing with lemon cream cheese frosting. Dust lightly with cinnamon and cut into small squares.

*Makes 20–24*

## GERMAN CINNAMON COOKIES

These cookies may take a little time and patience but are well worth the effort.

*200 g (7 oz, 1 ¾ cups) plain (all-purpose) flour*
*480 g (16 ½ oz, 4 ¼ cups) almonds, finely ground*
*390 g (14 oz, 2 cups) caster (superfine) sugar*
*5 x 60 g (2 oz) egg whites*
*320 g (11 oz, 1 ⅔ cups) icing (powdered) sugar*
*15 g (½ oz, 6 teaspoons) ground cinnamon*
*1 quantity royal icing (see page 156)*

Line baking trays (sheets) with baking parchment. Place all the ingredients into a mixing bowl and mix until a solid dough begins to form. If the mixture is too dry and will not form a dough, add additional egg white. If the mixture is too wet add extra icing sugar.

Remove from the bowl and place the dough onto a lightly floured surface. Roll out to approximately 1 cm (½ in) in thickness. Spread royal icing over the rolled base and place into the refrigerator for 1 hour to harden both dough and icing.

Preheat oven to 180°C (350°F). Using a floured cookie cutter, cut out star shapes and place each cookie onto the prepared tray. Bake in the preheated oven 10–15 minutes or until the icing begins to turn a golden brown.

*Makes 18–24*

OPPOSITE: *above, German Cinnamon Cookies; below, Gingerbread Squares*

# Vienna Cake

A *roaring log fire and snow outside are optional extras when serving this Yuletide favourite.*

150 g (5 ½ oz, ½ cup) clear honey
90 g (3 oz, ¼ cup) golden syrup (light treacle)
210 g (7 ½ oz, 1 ⅓ cups) soft (light) brown sugar
60 g (2 oz, ½ cup) plain (all-purpose) flour
60 g (2 oz, ½ cup) cocoa powder
2 teaspoons ground cinnamon
1 teaspoon mixed spice (see page 161)
120 g (4 oz, 1 cup) dried apricots, finely chopped
90 g (3 oz, ½ cup) glacé (candied) pineapple, finely chopped
150 g (5 ½ oz, 1 cup) mixed (candied) peel
180 g (6 ½ oz, 1 ½ cups) hazelnuts, finely chopped
150 g (5 ½ oz, 1 ⅓ cups) blanched (skinned) almonds, finely chopped
90 g (3 oz, ¾ cup) macadamia (Queensland) nuts, finely chopped
zest of 1 lemon
zest of 1 orange
1 tablespoon marmalade
icing (powdered) sugar for dusting

Preheat oven to 160°C (320°F). Lightly grease and line an 18 cm x 28 cm x 2 cm (7 in x 11 in x ¾ in) baking tray (sheet) with baking parchment.

Place the honey, golden syrup and brown sugar in a saucepan and bring slowly to the boil. Boil, stirring continuously, for 5 minutes. In a large mixing bowl, mix together the flour, cocoa, spices, fruits and nuts, lemon and orange zest and marmalade. Pour the boiled mixture over the top and stir until all are combined. Pour the mixture into the prepared tray and press flat using the back of a spoon. Bake in the preheated oven 25 minutes. Remove and dust heavily with icing sugar whilst still hot. Allow to cool for 40 minutes before cutting into very thin fingers to serve.

*Makes 28–30*

# Austrian Lebkuchen

T*his cookie has been made in Austria and Germany for centuries.*

60 g (2 oz, ¼ cup) unsalted butter
25 ml (1 fl oz, 1 ½ tablespoons) milk
240 g (8 ½ oz, ⅔ cup) clear honey or golden syrup (light treacle)
225 g (8 oz, 1 ¾ cups) plain (all-purpose) flour
2 tablespoons cornflour (US cornstarch)
1 teaspoon mixed spice (see page 161)
½ teaspoon cardamom
½ teaspoon ground cinnamon
15 g (½ oz, 2 tablespoons) cocoa powder
1 teaspoon bicarbonate of soda (baking soda)
2 tablespoons cornflour (US cornstarch), extra
1 tablespoon caster (superfine) sugar
1 tablespoon icing (powdered) sugar
2 tablespoons unsalted butter
300 g (10 ½ oz) dark (plain or semi-sweet) chocolate, melted (see page 160)

Place the butter, milk and honey in a saucepan and heat slowly, stirring constantly, until the mixture comes to the boil. Sift the flour, cornflour, spices, cocoa and bicarbonate of soda and add to the butter mixture. Stir until smooth then cover with plastic (cling) wrap and leave in a cool place for 2 hours. Place the cornflour, caster sugar and icing sugar in a bowl and mix well. Put to one side. Preheat oven to 180°C (350°F). Line baking trays (sheets) with baking parchment. Remove mixture from the saucepan and knead lightly on a floured surface. The mixture will feel stiff and gelatinous. Knead quickly and lightly being careful not to overwork the dough. Roll the mixture to 5 mm (¼ in) in thickness and using a floured, 5 cm (2 in) round cookie cutter, cut out rounds and place them onto the prepared tray. Roll any scrap pastry once only as the mixture will become overworked. Bake in the preheated oven 10–12 minutes. Remove and immediately brush rounds lightly with the extra butter and then dust with the cornflour, icing sugar and caster sugar mixture. When completely cold dip the bases in the melted chocolate and allow to set before serving.

*Makes 12–18*

OPPOSITE: *above, Vienna Cake; below, Austrian Lebkuchen*

# COCOA DIAMONDS

*Almonds and cocoa subtly combine in this recipe.*

*180 g (6 ½ oz, 1 ½ cups) plain (all-purpose) flour*
*1 teaspoon baking powder*
*30 g (1 oz, ¼ cup) cocoa powder*
*60 g (2 oz, ⅔ cup) desiccated (shredded) coconut*
*120 g (4 oz, ½ cup) caster (superfine) sugar*
*120 g (4 oz, ½ cup) unsalted butter*
*1 x 60 g (2 oz, large) egg*
*12–16 whole blanched (skinned) almonds*
*210 g (7 ½ oz, 2 cups) cocoa powder, extra, for dusting*

Preheat oven to 180°C (350°F). Grease a 19 cm x 28 cm x 2 cm (7 ½ in x 11 in x ¾ in) baking tray (sheet). Sift together the flour, baking powder and cocoa. Add the coconut and sugar and mix together well. Melt the butter in a saucepan. Add to the dry ingredients together with the egg. Mix well. Press the mixture into the prepared tray. Press whole blanched almonds at regular intervals over the surface of the mixture. Bake in the preheated oven 15 minutes. Cool in the tray before dusting with cocoa and cutting into diamond shapes.

*Makes 12–16*

# EASTER COOKIES

*Perfect not just at Easter but year round.*

*420 g (15 oz, 3 ⅓ cups) plain (all-purpose) flour*
*2 teaspoons baking powder*
*120 g (4 oz, ½ cup) caster (superfine) sugar*
*30 g (1 oz, ⅓ cup) desiccated (shredded) coconut*
*1 teaspoon ground cinnamon*
*150 g (5 ½ oz, ⅔ cup) unsalted butter*
*3 x 60 g (2 oz, large) eggs*
*60 g (2 oz, ⅓ cup) currants*
*30 g (1 oz, 2 tablespoons) glacé (candied) cherries, chopped*
*30 g (1 oz, 2 tablespoons) mixed (candied) peel*
*caster (superfine) sugar, extra, for dusting*

Preheat oven to 175°C (345°F). Line baking trays (sheets) with baking parchment. Place the flour, baking powder, sugar, coconut, cinnamon and butter in a mixing bowl and crumb the butter through the dry ingredients. Add the lightly beaten eggs and continue mixing until a dough starts to form. Add the currants, cherries and mixed peel and continue working to a dough. Roll out to 4 mm (¼ in) in thickness on a lightly floured surface and cut out 5 cm (2 in) squares. Place onto the prepared tray and bake in the preheated oven 10–12 minutes or until lightly golden brown. Dust with caster sugar whilst hot.

*Makes 36*

# APRICOT LEAVES

*Thin, crisp almond-flavoured cookies topped with apricot jam.*

*120 g (4 oz, ½ cup) caster (superfine) sugar*
*120 g (4 oz, ½ cup) unsalted butter*
*240 g (8 ½ oz) marzipan (see page 160)*
*1 x 60 g (2 oz, large) egg*
*270 g (9 ½ oz, 2 ¼ cups) plain (all-purpose) flour*
*1 quantity egg wash (see page 156)*
*210 g (7 ½ oz, 2 cups) flaked almonds*
*120 g (4 oz, ⅓ cup) apricot jam*

Preheat oven to 200°C (400°F). Line baking trays (sheets) with baking parchment. Place the sugar, butter and marzipan in a bowl and mix until well combined. Add the egg and flour and work the mixture to a dough. Roll out on a lightly floured bench to 4 mm (⅛ in) in thickness. Using a crimped or fluted round cookie cutter, cut 4 cm (2 in) diamond shapes from the dough. Egg wash each shape and sprinkle with flaked almonds. On the top of each place a dot of apricot jam. Place onto the prepared tray and bake in the preheated oven 8–10 minutes or until golden brown. Cool on the tray before serving.

*Makes 36*

OPPOSITE: *above left, Cocoa Diamonds; above right, Apricot Leaves; below, Easter Cookies*

# SPICE FINGERS

*Traditionally baked and served at Christmas, these fingers are best eaten the day they are made.*

*60 g (2 oz, ¼ cup) unsalted butter*
*25 ml (1 fl oz, 1 ½ tablespoons) milk*
*240 g (8 ½ oz, ⅔ cup) golden syrup (light treacle)*
*225 g (8 oz, 1 ¾ cups) plain (all-purpose) flour*
*1 teaspoon mixed spices (see page 161)*
*½ teaspoon ground cinnamon*
*1 teaspoon bicarbonate of soda (baking soda)*

### ICING GLAZE
*150 g (5 oz, 1 cup) icing (powdered) sugar*
*2 tablespoons lemon juice*

Line baking trays (sheets) with baking parchment. Place the butter, milk and golden syrup (light treacle) into a saucepan and heat gradually, stirring constantly, until the mixture comes to the boil. Sift the flour, spices and bicarbonate of soda and add to the butter mixture. Stir until smooth and then cover with plastic (cling) wrap and leave in a cool place for 2 hours. Preheat oven to 180°C (350°F). Remove mixture from the saucepan and knead lightly on a floured surface. Take tablespoons of dough and roll into a sausage shape, 1–1 ½ cm (½–¾ in) in thickness. Place onto the prepared tray allowing room for spreading and bake in the preheated oven 8–10 minutes. The fingers should be soft and golden brown. As soon as the fingers are removed from the oven, carefully brush the top of each with the lemon icing glaze. Allow to cool before serving.

### ICING GLAZE
Sift the icing sugar. Mix in the lemon juice to make a thin icing. If icing is too thick add extra lemon juice or warm water.

*Makes 24*

# AMERICAN THANKSGIVING PUMPKIN FINGERS

*This recipe keeps well stored in the refrigerater.*

*105 g (3 ½ oz, ¾ cup) plain (all-purpose) flour*
*45 g (1 ½ oz, 3 tablespoons) icing (powdered) sugar*
*60 g (2 oz, ¼ cup) unsalted butter*
*1 x 60 g (2 oz, large) egg yolk*

### FILLING
*240 g (8 ½ oz, 1 cup) single or light cream*
*2 x 60 g (2 oz, large) eggs*
*480 g (17 oz, 2 cups) cooked pumpkin*
*210 g (7 ½ oz, 1 ⅓ cups) soft (light) brown sugar*
*½ teaspoon ground cinnamon*
*½ teaspoon ground ginger*

Preheat oven to 175°C (345°F). Grease and line an 18 cm x 28 cm x 2 cm (7 in x 11 in x ¾ in) baking tray (sheet) with baking parchment. Place the flour and sugar in a bowl. Add the butter and lightly rub into the flour until mixture resembles dry breadcrumbs. Add the egg yolk and mix thoroughly. Turn the dough onto a lightly floured surface and knead lightly. Press the mixture into the prepared tray. Bake in the pre-heated oven 8–10 minutes or until golden brown. Maintain oven temperature. Pour the filling over the pre-baked base. Return to the oven and bake for a further 45–50 minutes or until a knife inserted comes out clean. Allow to cool completely before cutting into fingers.

### FILLING
Place all filling ingredients into a blender or food processor and blend or pureé until smooth.

*Makes 25*

## SCANDINAVIAN CHRISTMAS COOKIES

The mixture for this recipe is stored in the refrigerator 24 hours before baking.

*240 g (8 ½ oz, 1 cup) unsalted butter*
*210 g (7 ½ oz, 1 cup) caster (superfine) sugar*
*90 g (3 oz, ¼ cup) golden syrup (light treacle)*
*1 tablespoon honey*
*90 g (3 oz, ¾ cup) flaked almonds*
*15 g (½ oz, 6 teaspoons) ground cinnamon*
*1 ½ teaspoons ground cardamom*
*1 ½ teaspoons ground ginger*
*1 teaspoon bicarbonate of soda (baking soda)*
*1 tablespoon water*
*400 g (14 oz, 3 cups) plain (all-purpose) flour*

Place the butter, sugar, syrup, honey, almonds and spices in a saucepan and heat gently until the butter melts, stirring constantly. Bring to the boil and then remove from the heat, still stirring. Dissolve the soda in the water and add to the mixture. Add the flour and work to a dough. (This may require more or less flour depending on whether the dough is sticky or dry.) Allow dough to cool slightly. Knead lightly and then cut into two portions. Shape both pieces of dough into blocks 5 cm x 5 cm (2 in x 2 in). Wrap each block in plastic (cling) wrap and refrigerate for 24 hours. Preheat oven to 180°C (350°F). Line baking trays (sheets) with baking parchment. Remove the dough from plastic cling (wrap) and cut into very thin slices. Place each cookie onto the prepared tray and allow room for spreading. Bake in the preheated oven 10 minutes. Remove and allow to cool on the trays. Serve plain or dusted with icing sugar.

*Makes 36*

## ALMOND FINGERS

Sandwiched together with rich ganache filling, these fingers will brighten any festive occasion.

*3 x 60 g (2 oz, large) egg whites*
*60 g (2 oz, ¼ cup) caster (superfine) sugar*
*225 g (8 oz, 1 cup) caster (superfine) sugar, extra*
*225 g (8 oz, 2 cups) ground almonds*
*1 quantity ganache filling (see page 155)*

Preheat oven to 160°C (320°F). Line baking trays (sheets) with baking parchment.

Whisk the egg whites and the first amount of sugar until stiff peaks are formed (see page 159). Place the second amount of sugar and the ground almonds into a blender and grind together. Continue whisking the egg whites and slowly add the sugar and almonds until all the ingredients are mixed.

Using a 1 cm (½ in) plain round nozzle fitted to a piping (pastry) bag, pipe small 5 cm (2 in) fingers onto the prepared tray. Bake in the preheated oven 10–12 minutes or until lightly golden. Allow to cool on the tray. When cold join two fingers together with piped ganache filling.

*Makes 18–24*

OPPOSITE: *above, Almond Fingers; below, Scandinavian Christmas Cookies*

# WHITE CHRISTMAS

*C*opha and coconut provide the 'white' and glacé fruit the 'Christmas' in this delicious treat.

*60 g (2 oz, 2 ½ cups) rice bubbles (crispies)*
*45 g (1 ½ oz, ½ cup) desiccated (shredded) coconut*
*50 g (1 ¾ oz, ½ cup) macadamia (Queensland) nuts, chopped*
*60 g (2 oz, ⅓ cup) icing (powdered) sugar*
*50 g (1 ¾ oz, ⅓ cup) sultanas (golden raisins)*
*15 g (½ oz, 1 tablespoon) mixed (candied) peel*
*15 g (½ oz, 1 tablespoon) glacé (candied) cherries, chopped*
*30 g (1 oz, ¼ cup) dried apricots, chopped*
*150 g (5 oz) copha (white coconut shortening)*

Lightly grease and line a 19 cm x 28 cm x 2 cm (7 ½ in x 11 in x ¾ in) baking tray (sheet) with baking parchment.

Place the rice bubbles, coconut and chopped macadamias in a bowl and sift the icing sugar over them. Place the sultanas, mixed peel, chopped glacé cherries and apricots on top and combine well. Place the copha in a saucepan and melt over a gentle heat. Pour the copha over the dry ingredients and fruit and stir until combined. Do not overmix or crush the dried fruits. Spread the mixture into the prepared tray and smooth over. Place in the refrigerator for 1 hour before cutting into fingers and serving.

*Makes 20*

# LINZE LEAVES

*A* relative of the Linzer Torte, this is a European Christmas favourite.

*270 g (9 ½ oz, 2 ¼ cups) plain (all-purpose) flour*
*30 g (1 oz, 3 tablespoons) ground cinnamon*
*210 g (7 ½ oz, 1 cup) caster (superfine) sugar*
*150 g (5 ½ oz, 1 ⅓ cups) ground almonds*
*210 g (7 ½ oz, 1 cup) unsalted butter, cut into small pieces*
*1 x 60 g (2 oz, large) egg, lightly beaten*
*juice of 1 lemon*
*25 ml (1 fl oz, 1 ½ tablespoons) milk*
*milk chocolate, melted, to decorate (see page 160)*

Preheat oven to 180°C (350°F). Line the base of baking trays (sheets) with baking parchment.

Place the flour, cinnamon, sugar and ground almonds in a bowl and mix lightly. Add the butter and very lightly rub into the flour until the mixture resembles fresh breadcrumbs. Add the egg, lemon juice and enough of the milk to make a firm dough. Wrap in plastic (cling) wrap and place in the refrigerator for 1 hour.

Remove the pastry and knead lightly until ready to roll. Roll on a lightly floured surface to 4 mm (¼ in) in thickness and then, using a 5 cm (2 in) round cookie cutter, cut leaf shapes from the dough. Place onto the prepared trays and, using a sharp knife, make a line down the centre and down the sides to resemble leaf veins. Bake in the preheated oven 10–12 minutes or until cooked. Allow to cool in the tray. Dip one side into the melted chocolate and allow to set before serving.

*Makes 36*

# LIGHT
## *and*
# DELICIOUS

*Feather light and truly scrumptious.*

## MUESLI CRUNCH

Muesli was developed as a health food by a Swiss nutrionist at the end of the 19th century. These cookies are both healthy and delicious.

*180 g (6 ½ oz, ¾ cup) unsalted butter*
*240 g (8 ½ oz, 1 ¼ cups) caster (superfine) sugar*
*1 teaspoon ground cinnamon*
*240 g (8 ½ oz, 2 ¾ cups) rolled oats or muesli*
*60 g (2 oz, ½ cup) dried apricots, chopped*
*120 g (4 oz, 1 ⅓ cups) desiccated (shredded) coconut*

Preheat oven to 175°C (345°F). Grease and line a 19 cm x 28 cm x 2 cm (7 ½ in x 11 in x ¾ in) baking tray (sheet) with baking parchment.

Place the butter, sugar and cinnamon into a saucepan and melt over low heat. Stir the muesli, dried apricots and coconut into the melted butter mixture and press the mixture into the prepared tray.

Bake in the preheated oven 15 minutes. Remove and allow to cool before cutting into finger-sized portions.

*Makes 20*

## LEMON DELIGHTS

The lemon cream cheese frosting for these cookies will also soften them, so only ice as you need them.

*240 g (8 ½ oz, 1 cup) unsalted butter, softened*
*240 g (8 ½ oz, 2 cups) plain (all-purpose) flour, sifted*
*180 g (6 ½ oz, ¾ cup) caster (superfine) sugar*
*75 ml (2 ½ fl oz, ⅓ cup) milk*
*zest of 2 lemons*
*1 quantity lemon cream cheese frosting (see page 157)*

CINNAMON SUGAR
*120 g (4 oz, ½ cup) caster (superfine) sugar mixed with 1 tablespoon ground cinnamon*

Preheat oven to 180°C (350°F). Place the butter in a mixing bowl and beat until almost white in colour and light and creamy in texture. Add half the flour, all of the sugar, milk and lemon zest. Mix until well combined. Add remaining flour and stir in by hand until all is mixed. Place teaspoonfuls of the mixture onto an ungreased baking tray (sheet). Leave 2–3 cm (1 in) between each cookie to allow for spreading. Bake in the preheated oven 10–12 minutes or until just golden brown. Remove from the tray and cool on a wire rack. Ice with lemon frosting and dust lightly with a sprinkling of cinnamon sugar.

*Makes 36*

OPPOSITE: *above, Lemon Delights; below, Muesli Crunch*

# CITRUS TWISTS

*Bite through the refreshing citrus glaze into a delightfully crisp biscuit.*

*210 g (7 ½ oz, 1 ¾ cups) plain (all-purpose) flour*
*1 tablespoon baking powder*
*60 g (2 oz, ¼ cup) unsalted butter*
*90 g (3 oz, ⅓ cup) caster (superfine) sugar*
*juice and zest of 1 lemon*
*zest of 1 orange*
*1 x 60 g (2 oz, large) egg*

ICING GLAZE
*150 g (5 ½ oz, 1 cup) icing (powdered) sugar, sifted*
*1 tablespoon lemon juice*
*1 tablespoon orange juice*
*¼ tablespoon lemon zest*
*¼ tablespoon orange zest*

Place the sifted flour, baking powder, butter and sugar into a mixing bowl. Rub the butter into the dry ingredients until mixture resembles fine bread-crumbs. Add the lemon juice, lemon and orange zest and egg to the mixture and continue mixing until a smooth dough has formed. Wrap the dough in plastic (cling) wrap and refrigerate for 30 minutes.

Preheat oven to 180°C (350°F). Line baking trays (sheets) with baking parchment. Remove dough from the refrigerator and lightly knead on a floured surface. Take teaspoonfuls of the mixture and roll into 10 cm (4 in) lengths. (Two lengths are required for each twist.) Sit two lengths side by side and press the top ends together. Then twist the two together, pressing the ends together again at the finish. Trim the ends and cut each twist in half. Place the twists onto the prepared trays and bake in the preheated oven 8–10 minutes or until lightly golden brown. Remove from the oven and carefully place the twists onto a wire rack. Spoon small amounts of the pre-pared icing mixture over each twist whilst still hot. Allow to cool and set before serving.

ICING GLAZE
Place the sifted icing sugar in a bowl. Add the juices and zest and mix until smooth.

*Makes 12–18*

**STEP ONE:** *Sit two lengths side by side and press the top ends together.*

**STEP TWO:** *Twist the two lengths together.*

**STEP THREE:** *Trim the ends and cut each twist in half.*

# ORANGE SYRUP SQUARES

*The word 'orange' derives from the Tamil word meaning 'fragrant'. Enjoy both the fragrance and flavour in these delicious fingers.*

*240 g (8 ½ oz, 1 cup) unsalted butter*
*350 g (12 oz, 2 cups) soft (light) brown sugar*
*100 g (3 ½ oz, ¼ cup) golden syrup (light treacle)*
*zest of 2 oranges*
*juice of 1 orange*
*400 g (14 oz, 3 cups) plain (all-purpose) flour*
*1 tablespoon baking powder*
*3 x 60 g (2 oz, large) eggs*
*1 quantity of orange frosting (see page 157)*

Preheat oven to 180°C (350°F). Line a 25 cm x 30 cm x 3 cm (10 in x 12 in x 1 ¼ in) baking tray (sheet) with baking parchment.

Place the butter, sugar, syrup, orange zest and juice in a saucepan and melt gradually. Slowly bring the mixture to the boil. Pour the boiling mixture into the bowl with the sifted flour and baking powder. Stir until well combined and when cool, add the eggs. Mix well. Pour into the prepared tray.

Bake in the preheated oven for 25–30 minutes. Allow to cool in the tray before decorating with orange frosting. Cut into squares.

*Makes 24*

# DATE AND LEMON FINGERS

*Dates are a good source of protein and iron and combine well with the lemon in this recipe.*

*100 ml (3 ½ fl oz, ½ cup) water*
*juice and zest of 2 lemons*
*2 teaspoons caster (superfine) sugar*
*1 teaspoon ground cinnamon*
*330 g (11 ½ oz, 2 cups) dry or semi-dry dates, stoned (pitted)*
*240 g (8 ½ oz, 1 cup) unsalted butter*
*240 g (8 ½ oz, 1 ¼ cups) caster (superfine) sugar, extra*
*2 x 60 g (2 oz, large) eggs*
*420 g (15 oz, 3 ⅓ cups) plain (all-purpose) flour*
*4 teaspoons baking powder*
*pinch salt*
*1 quantity egg wash (see page 156)*

Preheat oven to 180°C (350°F). Lightly grease a 19 cm x 28 cm x 2 cm (7 ½ in x 11 in x ¾ in) baking tray (sheet). Place the water, lemon juice and zest, sugar and cinnamon in a small saucepan and bring to the boil. Whilst boiling add the stoned dates and continue to simmer for 10 minutes or until the dates are quite soft. Remove from the heat and allow to cool. Place the butter and extra sugar in a mixing bowl and cream together until light and fluffy. Add the eggs and beat well. Add the sifted flour, baking powder and salt. Work in the flour until a dough is formed. Turn this out of the mixing bowl and knead into a single mass. Cut into two equal pieces. Press one half of the dough into the prepared tray. Spread this with the date and lemon mixture. Gently press the remaining dough over the top. Lightly egg wash the top of the pastry and score lightly using a fork. Bake in the preheated oven 35–40 minutes before removing to cool in the tray. Cut into fingers when cold.

*Makes 24*

OPPOSITE: *above, Orange Syrup Squares; below, Date and Lemon Fingers*

# HAZELNUT SHORTBREADS

*A crisp, light shortbread, delicately flavoured with hazelnuts and served in bite-sized pieces.*

*510 g (18 oz, 4 cups) plain (all-purpose) flour*
*330 g (11 ½ oz, 1 ⅓ cups) unsalted butter*
*180 g (6 ½ oz, ¾ cup) caster (superfine) sugar*
*1 x 60 g (2 oz, large) egg yolk*
*120 g (4 oz, 1 ¼ cups) ground hazelnuts*
*icing (powdered) sugar, for dusting*

Place the flour, butter and sugar in a mixing bowl and rub the butter through the dry ingredients until the mixture resembles coarse breadcrumbs. Add the egg yolk and continue mixing until a dough is formed. Add the ground hazelnuts and mix through the dough quickly, being careful not to overwork the dough. Wrap in plastic (cling) wrap and refrigerate for 30 minutes.

Preheat oven to 180°C (350°F). Line baking trays (sheets) with baking parchment. Remove the dough from the refrigerator and knead very lightly until soft enough to roll. On a lightly floured surface, roll into a large square or rectangular shape 1 cm (½ in) thick. Using a sharp knife cut into 5–8 cm (2–3 in) strips. Slide a palette under several of the strips simultaneously, and place carefully on the prepared tray. Leave 2–3 cm (1 in) between each shortbread to allow for spreading. Bake in the preheated oven 10–12 minutes or until lightly golden brown. Dust with icing sugar whilst still hot and then allow to cool on the tray before serving.

*Makes 58*

# ICED COCONUT FINGERS

*A delicate blend of crisp coconut and refreshing citrus.*

*120 g (4 oz, ½ cup) unsalted butter*
*90 g (3 oz, ⅓ cup) caster (superfine) sugar*
*juice and zest of 1 lemon*
*1 x 60 g (2 oz, large) egg*
*210 g (7 ½ oz, 1 ¾ cups) plain (all-purpose) flour*
*45 g (1 ½ oz, 5 tablespoons) custard powder (cornstarch or English Dessert Powder)*
*120 g (4 oz, 1 ⅓ cups) desiccated (shredded) coconut*

### LEMON ICING
*240 g (8 ½ oz, 1 ½ cups) icing (powdered) sugar*
*60 g (2 oz, ¼ cup) unsalted butter, melted*
*juice and zest of 1 lemon*

Preheat oven to 180°C (350°F). Line baking trays (sheets) with baking parchment. Place the butter, sugar and lemon zest in a mixing bowl and cream until light and fluffy. Add the egg and beat until combined. Stir in the lemon juice, sifted flour and custard powder, then the coconut. Take small, equal amounts of the mixture and roll into long fingers. Place onto the prepared tray and bake in the preheated oven 12–15 minutes or until golden brown. Cool on a wire rack and then pour over the lemon icing.

### LEMON ICING
Sift the icing sugar into a bowl. Stir in the melted butter and lemon juice and stir over hot water until smooth.

*Makes 24*

OPPOSITE: *above, Hazelnut Shortbreads; below, Iced Coconut Fingers*

# MIDNIGHT LACE

*Light, thin and lacy, these crisp delights will have you up at midnight raiding the cookie jar.*

120 g (4 oz, ¹/₂ cup) unsalted butter
120 g (4 oz, ¹/₂ cup) caster (superfine) sugar
30 g (1 oz, 2 tablespoons) thickened (double or heavy) cream
pinch ground cinnamon
90 g (3 oz, ³/₄ cup) macadamia (Queensland) nuts, finely ground
60 g (2 oz, ¹/₂ cup) plain (all-purpose) flour
60 g (2 oz, ¹/₃ cup) icing (powdered) sugar, for dusting
1 ¹/₂ teaspoons ground cinnamon, extra, for dusting

Preheat oven to 180°C (350°F). Lightly grease baking trays (sheets). Place the butter, sugar, cream, cinnamon and nuts in a saucepan and slowly bring to the boil, stirring continuously. When mixture boils add the flour and keep stirring until well combined, without removing pan from the heat. Cook for 4 minutes, stirring continuously. Remove pan from heat and allow to cool slightly. Drop spoonfuls of the mixture onto the prepared trays, allowing room for spreading. Bake in the preheated oven 5–8 minutes. Allow to cool slightly on the tray. Drape each cookie over a lightly oiled wooden spoon or any other utensil that will curve the cookie into a hollow tube shape. Allow to cool. Mix the icing sugar and cinnamon together and dust cookies before serving.

*Makes 12–16*

# JAMAICAN RUMBA SQUARES

*Caribbean delights with the crisp flavour of fresh citrus and coconut.*

150 g (5 ¹/₂ oz, ²/₃ cup) unsalted butter, softened
240 g (8 ¹/₂ oz, 1 ¹/₄ cups) caster (superfine) sugar
3 x 60 g (2 oz, large) eggs
310 g (11 oz, 2 ¹/₂ cups) plain (all-purpose) flour
1 tablespoon baking powder
75 g (2 ¹/₂ oz, ¹/₂ cup) cornflour (US cornstarch)
75 ml (2 ¹/₂ fl oz, ¹/₃ cup) white or brown rum
120 g (4 oz, 1 ¹/₃ cups) desiccated (shredded) coconut
juice and zest of 2 lemons
juice and zest of 1 orange
desiccated (shredded) coconut, extra, for decorating

Preheat oven to 180°C (350°F). Lightly grease and line a 25 cm x 19 cm x 2 cm (10 in x 7 ½ in x ¾ in) baking tray (sheet) with baking parchment. Place the butter and sugar into a mixing bowl and beat until light and fluffy. Add the eggs one at a time and beat well after each addition. Fold the rum through the mixture until well combined. Sift the flour, baking powder and cornflour together and add to the mixture together with the coconut and lemon and orange juice and zest. Spread the mixture into the prepared tray and sprinkle with the coconut. Bake in the preheated oven 45–50 minutes or until firm to the touch. Remove from the oven and allow to cool in the tray. Cut into squares.

*Makes 20*

# FIG AND ALMOND COOKIES

*Figs were an early symbol of peace and prosperity. You might find your own sense of well-being from these delicious cookies!*

210 g , 1 ³/₄ cups (all-purpose) flour
1 teaspoon baking powder
120 g (4 oz, ¹/₂ cup) butter
180 g (6 ¹/₂ oz, ³/₄ cup) caster (superfine) sugar
1 x 60 g (2 oz, large) egg
60 g (2 oz, ¹/₂ cup) slivered almonds
90 g (3 oz, ¹/₂ cup) dried figs, chopped

Preheat oven to 180°C (350°F). Lightly grease two baking trays (sheets). Sift the flour and baking powder. Cream the butter and sugar until light and fluffy. Add the egg and combine well. Fold in the flour, baking powder, almonds and figs and mix together. Drop tablespoonfuls of the mixture onto the prepared trays and bake in the preheated oven 12–15 minutes. Remove from trays and cool on a wire rack.

*Makes 36*

OPPOSITE: *above, Fig and Almond Cookies; centre, Midnight Lace; below, Jamaican Rumba Squares*

# COCONUT SHORTIES

*Light and buttery shortbreads with the added crunch of coconut.*

150 g (5 ½ oz, ⅔ cup) unsalted butter, softened
120 g (4 oz, ⅓ cup) golden syrup (light treacle)
2 x 60 g (2 oz, large) egg yolks
210 g (7 ½ oz, 1 ¾ cups) plain (all-purpose) flour
120 g (4 oz, 1 ⅓ cups) desiccated (shredded) coconut
60 g (2 oz, 2 tablespoons) strawberry jam

### TOPPING

2 x 60 g (2 oz, large) egg whites
210 g (7 ½ oz, 1 ¼ cups) icing (powdered) sugar
150 g (5 ½ oz, 1 ⅔ cups) desiccated (shredded) coconut

Preheat oven to 145°C (290°F). Grease and line a 18 cm x 28 cm x 2 cm (7 in x 11 in x ¾ in) baking tray (sheet) with baking parchment. Place the butter, golden syrup and egg yolks together in a bowl and work in the flour and coconut. Press into the prepared tray. Spread with the strawberry jam. Spread the topping over the jam-covered base. Bake in the preheated oven 45 minutes. While still warm cut into fingers.

### TOPPING

Beat the egg whites until they form stiff peaks (see page 159). Slowly add the icing sugar whilst still whisking. Fold through the coconut.

*Makes 20*

# LEMON CHEESECAKE SQUARES

*These squares are a wonderful variation on the traditional cheesecake.*

240 g (8 ½ oz, 2 ¼ cups) sweet plain biscuit (cookie) crumbs
120 g (4 oz, ½ cup) unsalted butter, melted
360 g (12 ½ oz, 1 ½ cups) cream cheese
150 g (5 ½ oz, ⅔ cup) caster (superfine) sugar
2 x 60 g (2 oz, large) eggs
6 level teaspoons gelatine (gelatin)
120 ml (4 fl oz, ½ cup) cold water
juice of 1 lemon
zest of 2 lemons, grated
300 ml (10 ½ fl oz, 1 ¼ cups) thickened (double or heavy) cream, whipped
ground cinnamon, for dusting

Line a 25 cm x 30 cm x 3 cm (10 in x 12 in x 1 ¼ in) baking tray (sheet) with plastic (cling) wrap. Mix together the biscuit crumbs and butter and press the mixture over the base of the tray. Press firmly in place with the back of a spoon. Place in the refrigerator for 1 hour. Beat the cream cheese and sugar together until light and creamy. Beat in the eggs, one at a time. Mix the gelatine in the cold water in a small bowl and let stand for 3 minutes. Heat the lemon juice until just boiling and add the soaked gelatine. Remove from heat and stir until gelatine dissolves. Add zest and cool. Beat into the creamed ingredients. Gently fold in by hand the whipped cream. Pour into the chilled crust and refrigerate for at least 2 hours or until set. Dust lightly with cinnamon and cut into squares with a hot knife.

*Makes 20*

OPPOSITE: *above, Coconut Shorties; below, Lemon Cheesecake Squares*

# BAKED LEMON FINGERS

*Topped with delicious lemon cream cheese frosting.*

120 g (4 oz, ½ cup) unsalted butter
120 g (4 oz, ¾ cup) soft (light) brown sugar
180 g (6 ½ oz, 1 ½ cups) plain (all-purpose) flour

### FILLING
2 x 60 g (2 oz, large) eggs
150 g (5 ½ oz, 1 cup) soft (light) brown sugar
180 g (6 ½ oz, 2 cups) desiccated (shredded) coconut
210 g (7 ½ oz, 1 ¾ cups) walnuts, chopped
60 g (2 oz, ½ cup) plain (all-purpose) flour
½ teaspoon vanilla essence (extract)
juice and zest of 2 lemons
1 quantity lemon cream cheese frosting (see page 157)

Preheat oven to 140°C (285°F). Grease and line an 18 cm x 28 cm x 2 cm (7 in x 11 in x ¾ in) baking tray (sheet) with baking parchment. Cream the butter and sugar together until light and creamy. Add the flour and mix until all is combined. Press the mixture into the prepared tray. Bake in the preheated oven 10 minutes. Remove base from oven and increase temperature to 180°C (350°F). Spread the filling evenly over the precooked base and place into the hotter oven for 20 minutes. Allow to cool in the tray and then spread with Lemon Cream Cheese Frosting before cutting into fingers.

### FILLING
Place the eggs in a mixing bowl and lightly whisk. Add the brown sugar, coconut, walnuts, flour, vanilla and lemon zest and juice. Mix well.

*Makes 25–30*

# COCONUT SQUARES

*Orange zest gives a special tangy flavour to this recipe.*

180 g (6 ½ oz, 1 ½ cups) plain (all-purpose) flour, sifted
90 g (3 oz, ½ cup) icing (powdered) sugar
100 g (3 ½ oz, ⅓ cup) unsalted butter, cut into small pieces
1 x 60 g (2 oz, large) egg yolk

### FILLING
240 g (8 ½ oz, 1 ¼ cups) caster (superfine) sugar
270 g (9 ½ oz, 2 ¾ cups) desiccated (shredded) coconut
zest of 2 oranges, grated
5 x 60 g (2 oz, large) egg whites

**1 quantity orange buttercream (see page 154)**

Lightly grease and line a 19 cm x 28 cm x 3 cm (7 ½ in x 11 in x 1 ¼ in) baking tray (sheet) with baking parchment. Place the flour, icing sugar and butter in a mixing bowl and lightly crumb the butter through the other ingredients until the mixture resembles coarse breadcrumbs. Add the egg yolk and rub through the mixture to form a dough. Wrap the dough in plastic (cling) wrap and refrigerate for 1 hour. Preheat oven to 175°C (345°F). Remove the dough from the refrigerator and roll out on a lightly floured surface to line the base of the tray. Pour the coconut mixture over the top and spread out evenly using a spatula or palette knife. Bake in the preheated oven 20–25 minutes or until the pastry and the coconut are golden brown. Remove from the oven and allow to cool in the tray. When cold, cover with orange buttercream and cut into squares.

### FILLING
Mix the sugar and coconut together and add the orange zest and lightly beaten egg whites. Mix with a wooden spoon for 2–3 minutes or until all the ingredients are well combined and quite moist.

*Makes 16–20*

OPPOSITE: *above, Coconut Squares; below, Baked Lemon Fingers*

# QUICK and EASY

*Easy and delicious recipes — great to make when you're in a rush or let children try them.*

## CHOCOLATE HEDGEHOG

**I**f this recipe was any easier you would simply eat the ingredients.

*420 g (15 oz, 3 ⅔ cups) plain sweet biscuits (cookies), crushed*
*210 g (7 ½ oz, 1 cup) unsalted butter*
*210 g (7 ½ oz, 1 cup) caster (superfine) sugar*
*60 g (2 oz, ⅔ cup) desiccated (shredded) coconut*
*60 g (2 oz, ½ cup) cocoa powder, sifted*
*3 x 60 g (2 oz, large) eggs, lightly beaten*
*1 quantity of chocolate frosting (see page 158)*
*chopped nuts or chocolate chips (drops) for decoration*

Lightly grease a 19 cm x 28 cm x 2 cm (7 ½ in x 11 in x ¾ in) baking tray (sheet). Place the crushed biscuits in a mixing bowl. Place the butter, sugar, coconut and cocoa in a saucepan and melt over a low heat. Bring to the boil and boil for 2 minutes. Remove from the heat and allow to cool. (At this stage the mixture may seem to separate. The eggs will bring the mixture together once more.) Whisk in the beaten eggs. Pour this mixture over the crushed biscuits and stir with a wooden spoon until all ingredients are well combined. Pour into the prepared tray and place in the refrigerator to cool. Remove from the refrigerator and spread with the chocolate frosting. Sprinkle with chopped nuts or chocolate chips. Cut into squares.

*Makes 16–20*

## HAZELNUT SQUARES

**T**his recipe combines the rich flavours of brown sugar, golden syrup and hazelnuts.

*240 g (8 ½ oz, 1 cup) unsalted butter*
*480 g (17 oz, 3 cups) soft (light) brown sugar*
*90 g (3 oz, ¼ cup) golden syrup (light treacle)*
*180 g (6 ½ oz, 1 ½ cups) hazelnuts, chopped*
*360 g (12 ½ oz, 3 cups) plain (all-purpose) flour*
*1 tablespoon baking powder*
*3 x 60 g (2 oz, large) eggs*
*1 quantity chocolate buttercream (see page 154)*
*roasted hazelnuts, chopped, extra, for decorating*

Preheat oven to 180°C (350°F). Line a 25 cm x 30 cm x 3 cm (10 in x 12 in x 1 ¼ in) baking tray (sheet) with baking parchment.

Place the butter, sugar, syrup and nuts in a saucepan and melt gradually. Slowly bring the mixture to the boil. Pour the boiling mixture into a bowl with the sifted flour and baking powder. Stir until well combined and when cool add the eggs. Mix well. Pour into the prepared pan. Bake in the preheated oven 25–30 minutes. Cool in the tray, before decorating with chocolate buttercream and extra chopped hazelnuts. Cut into squares.

*Makes 24*

OPPOSITE: *above, Hazelnut Squares; below, Chocolate Hedgehog*

# YO-YOS

*All these cookies are missing is a string around the middle!*

270 g (9 ½ oz, 1 cup) unsalted butter
90 g (3 oz, ½ cup) icing (powdered) sugar
90 g (3 oz, ⅔ cup) custard powder (cornstarch or English Dessert Powder)
270 g (9 ½ oz, 2 ¼ cups) plain (all-purpose) flour

### BUTTER FILLING
180 g (6 oz, 1 cup) icing (powdered) sugar
90 g (3 oz, ⅓ cup) unsalted butter
zest of 1 orange

Preheat oven to 175°C (345°F). Line baking trays (sheets) with baking parchment. Place the butter and sifted icing sugar in a mixing bowl and cream until light and fluffy. Sift the custard powder and flour together several times and then add to the creamed butter/sugar mixture. Mix until well combined. Take tablespoonfuls of the mixture and roll into balls. Place each ball onto the prepared tray and then lightly press with a flour-dusted fork to flatten. Bake in the preheated oven 18–20 minutes or until slightly brown. Allow to cool on the tray before joining two of the biscuits together with the butter filling.

### BUTTER FILLING
Place the sifted icing sugar, softened butter and orange zest in a bowl and mix together until the mixture is smooth and easily spread. Do not cream this mixture.

*Makes 18*

# CHOCOLATE FINGERS

*A quickly made treat for those in need of an immediate chocolate 'fix'.*

180 g (6 ½ oz, ¾ cup) unsalted butter
150 g (5 ½ oz, 1 ¼ cups) plain (all-purpose) flour
1 teaspoon baking powder
90 g (3 oz, 1 cup) desiccated (shredded) coconut
120 g (4 oz, ½ cup) caster (superfine) sugar
30 g (1 oz, ¼ cup) cocoa powder

### ICING
150 g (5 ½ oz, 1 cup) icing (powdered) sugar
15 g (½ oz, 2 tablespoons) cocoa powder
sufficient water to make a soft paste

desiccated (shredded) coconut, extra, for decoration

Preheat oven to 175°C (345°F). Grease an 18 cm x 28 cm x 2 cm (7 in x 11 in x ¾ in) baking tray (sheet). Place the butter in a saucepan and melt. Mix all the dry ingredients together in a mixing bowl and then add the melted butter. Mix well. Place the mixture immediately into the prepared tray and press in firmly. Bake in the preheated oven 20 minutes. Remove from the oven and ice immediately with the chocolate icing. Sprinkle with coconut and allow to cool. Cut into finger-sized portions.

### ICING
Sift together the icing sugar and cocoa powder and mix well. Add small amounts of water at a time and mix thoroughly between each addition. The icing mix should be thick enough so that it holds its shape for a few seconds when drizzled.

*Makes 16–20*

OPPOSITE: *above, Chocolate Fingers; below, Yo-Yos*

# DATE COOKIES

*Look for plump, moist dates to create a truly superb cookie.*

*180 g (6 ½ oz, 1 cup) soft (light) brown sugar*
*60 g (2 oz, 2 tablespoons) golden syrup (light treacle)*
*240 g (8 ½ oz, 1 cup) unsalted butter (softened)*
*2 x 60 g (2 oz, large) eggs*
*375 g (13 oz, 3 cups) plain (all-purpose) flour*
*1 tablespoon baking powder*
*120 g (4 oz, ¾ cup) soft dates, stoned (pitted) and chopped*
*caster (superfine) sugar, for dusting*

Preheat oven to 175°C (345°F). Line baking trays with baking parchment. Place the brown sugar, golden syrup and butter in a mixing bowl and cream until light and fluffy. Add the eggs slowly and ensure that the mixture is well combined between additions. Sift the flour and baking powder and add to the mixture with the chopped dates. Mix until smooth. Place teaspoonfuls of the mixture onto the prepared trays, allowing room for spreading. Bake in the preheated oven 15–18 minutes, or until lightly golden brown. Remove from the oven and immediately sprinkle with caster sugar.

*Makes 30*

# AMERICAN CORNFLAKE COOKIES

*The ever-popular cornflake becomes a delicious feature of these crunchy cookies.*

*600 g (21 oz) cornflakes*
*225 g (8 oz, 1 cup) unsalted butter, softened*
*180 g (6 ½ oz, 1 cup) soft (light) brown sugar*
*225 g (8 oz, 1 cup) caster (superfine) sugar*
*4 x 60 g (2 oz) eggs*
*315 g (11 oz, 2 ½ cups) plain (all-purpose) flour*
*1 teaspoon bicarbonate of soda (baking soda)*
*1 teaspoon baking powder*
*210 g (7 ½ oz, 2 ⅓ cups) flaked (shredded) coconut*

Preheat oven to 180°C (350°F). Line baking trays (sheets) with baking parchment. Place the cornflakes in a flat dish. Place the softened butter, brown sugar, and caster sugar in a mixing bowl and cream together until light and fluffy. Add the eggs slowly and combine well after each addition. Sift the flour, bicarbonate of soda and baking powder together and add to the mixture along with the coconut. Continue mixing until smooth (2–3 minutes). Drop table-spoonfuls of the mixture into the cornflakes and roll into balls. Place each ball onto the prepared tray allowing room for spreading. Bake in the preheated oven 15–20 minutes or until lightly golden brown.

*Makes 36*

# FLAP JACK FINGERS

*Popular as a sustaining treat with the pioneers of North America.*

*120 g (4 oz, ⅓ cup) golden syrup (light treacle)*
*180 g (6 ½ oz, ¾ cup) unsalted butter*
*30 g (1 oz, 1 tablespoon) clear honey*
*90 g (3 oz, ½ cup) soft (light) brown sugar*
*60 g (2 oz, ¼ cup) raw cane sugar*
*540 g (19 oz, 6 cups) rolled oats*

Preheat oven to 180°C (350°F). Grease and line an 18 cm x 28 cm x 2 cm (7 in x 11 in x ¾ in) baking tray (sheet) with baking parchment. Place the golden syrup, butter, honey and brown sugar in a saucepan and heat until the butter is melted. Pour this mixture over the raw sugar and oats and stir until well combined. Press the mixture into the prepared tray and score lightly with a knife into serving portions. Bake in the preheated oven 20–25 minutes. Allow to cool and cut.

*Makes 20–24*

OPPOSITE: *above, Flap Jack Fingers; centre, American Cornflake Cookies; below, Date Cookies*

# FIG AND GINGER FINGERS

*F*igs *are not only a good source of iron, calcium and phosphorus — they're also delicious in these lightly spiced fingers.*

*390 g (13 ½ oz, 1 ¾ cups) unsalted butter*
*360 g (12 ½ oz, 1 cup) golden syrup (light treacle)*
*1 x 60 g (2 oz, large) egg, lightly beaten*
*180 g (6 ½ oz, 1 cup) soft (light) brown sugar*
*390 g (13 ½ oz, 3 cups) plain (all-purpose) flour*
*1 ½ teaspoons bicarbonate soda (baking soda)*
*1 ½ teaspoons ground ginger*
*1 ½ teaspoons ground cinnamon*
*125 ml (4 ½ fl oz, ½ cup) boiling water*
*30 g (1 oz, 2 tablespoons) sour cream*
*210 g (7 ½ oz, 1 ⅓ cups) dried (crystallised) figs, chopped*

Preheat oven to 180°C (350°F). Grease and line a 25 cm x 30 cm x 3 cm (10 in x 12 in x 1 ¼ in) baking tray (sheet) with baking parchment.

Place the butter and syrup into a saucepan and heat slowly until melted. Add the egg and sugar, stirring continuously. Sift the flour, bicarbonate of soda and the spices together into a bowl. Add the egg mixture and water to the dry ingredients and mix quickly until smooth. Add the sour cream and the figs and stir through. Spread the mixture into the prepared tray and bake in the preheated oven 25–35 minutes or until a skewer inserted into the centre comes out clean. Cool in the tray before cutting into fingers.

*Makes 24*

# CHOCOLATE JEWEL FINGERS

*T*he *glowing colours of glacé fruits combine with nuts and cocoa in this rich bar.*

*60 g (2 oz, ½ cup) plain (all-purpose) flour*
*1 level teaspoon baking powder*
*45 g (1 ½ oz, ⅓ cup) cocoa powder*
*100 g (3 ½ oz, ½ cup) glacé (candied) ginger*
*100 g (3 ½ oz, ½ cup) glacé (candied) pineapple*
*120 g (4 oz, ⅔ cup) glacé (candied) red cherries*
*90 g (3 oz, ½ cup) glacé (candied) green cherries*
*100 g (3 ½ oz, ½ cup) sultanas (golden raisins)*
*120 g (4 oz, ¾ cup) stoned (pitted) dates*
*90 g (3 oz, ½ cup) mixed (candied) peel*
*60 g (2 oz, ⅔ cup) whole walnuts, halved*
*90 g (3 oz, ½ cup) whole brazil nuts*
*30 g (1 oz, ¼ cup) whole hazelnuts*
*60 g (2 oz, ½ cup) whole blanched almonds*
*60 g (2 oz, ⅓ cup) whole pecan nuts, halved*
*90 g (3 oz, ⅓ cup) caster (superfine) sugar*
*3 x 60 g (2 oz, large) eggs, beaten*

Preheat oven to 160°C (320°F). Grease an 18 cm x 28 cm x 2 cm (7 in x 11 in x ¾ in) baking tray (sheet) and line the base and sides of the tray with two thicknesses of baking parchment which sits 1–2 cm (½ –1 in) higher than the sides of the tray. Sift the flour, baking powder and cocoa together. Place all the fruits and nuts in a bowl. Mix the sifted flour and sugar into the fruit and nuts and then add the beaten eggs. Spoon the mixture into the prepared tray and spread until smooth. Bake in the preheated oven 40 minutes or until a skewer inserted into the centre comes out clean. Cool in the tray before dusting the top with icing sugar. When cool cut into very small fingers to serve.

*Makes 24*

OPPOSITE: *above, Chocolate Jewel Fingers; below, Fig and Ginger Fingers*

# DRIED FRUIT FINGERS

A *hint of Christmas all year round with this adaptation of a light fruit cake.*

120 g (4 oz, ½ cup) unsalted butter
75 g (2 ½ oz, ⅓ cup) icing (powdered) sugar
150 g (5 ½ oz, 1 ¼ cups) plain (all-purpose) flour

### FILLING
60 g (2 oz, ½ cup) dried apricots, finely chopped
60 g (2 oz, ⅓ cup) currants
60 g (2 oz, ⅓ cup) sultanas (golden raisins)
30 g (1 oz, 2 tablespoons) mixed (candied) peel
30 g (1 oz, 2 tablespoons) glacé (candied) cherries, chopped
50 ml (2 fl oz, ¼ cup) brandy
3 x 60 g (2 oz, large) eggs
120 g (4 oz, ¾ cup) soft (light) brown sugar
60 g (2 oz, ½ cup) plain (all-purpose) flour, sifted
1 teaspoon baking powder
150 g (5 oz, 1 ⅔ cups) desiccated (shredded) coconut

Preheat oven to 180°C (350°F). Grease and line a 25 cm x 30 cm x 3 cm (10 in x 12 in x 1 ¼ in) baking tray (sheet) with baking parchment. Place all ingredients in a mixing bowl and beat until soft. Spread the mixture over the base of the prepared tray and bake in the preheated oven 8–10 minutes or until lightly golden brown. Spread the filling over the pre-baked base and bake for a further 30–35 minutes or until firm to the touch. Allow to cool in the tray before cutting into fingers.

### FILLING
Soak the currants, apricots, sultanas, cherries and mixed peel in the brandy. Place the eggs and sugar in a mixing bowl and whisk until ribbon stage (see page 159). Fold the fruit, flour, baking powder and coconut into the egg mixture.

*Makes 16*

# DREAMY COCONUT TRIANGLES

E *asy to make and requiring no baking.*

520 g (18 ½ oz, 4 ¾ cups) plain sweet biscuits (cookies)
400 g (14 oz, 1 ¾ cup) sweetened condensed milk
240 g (8 ½ oz, 2 ⅔ cups) desiccated (shredded) coconut
200 g (7 oz, 1 cup) unsalted butter
1 teaspoon vanilla essence (extract)
100 g (3 ½ oz, ½ cup) glacé (candied) cherries
75 g (2 ½ oz, ½ cup) flaked almonds

### ORANGE ICING
240 g (8 ½ oz, 1 ½ cups) icing (powdered) sugar
30 g (1 oz, 2 tablespoons) unsalted butter
juice and zest of 1 large orange

30 g (1 oz, ⅓ cup) shredded (flaked) coconut, extra, for decoration

Grease a 25 cm x 30 cm x 3 cm (10 in x 12 in x 1 ¼ in) baking tray (sheet). Crush the biscuits to rough but fine crumbs. Place the condensed milk and the coconut in a bowl with the biscuit crumbs, glacé cherries and almonds and mix lightly by hand to combine. Place the butter in a saucepan and heat slowly until melted. Add the melted butter and vanilla essence to the mixture and work all ingredients together until well mixed. Press the mixture into the prepared tray and smooth using the back of a spoon. Place in the refrigerator for 1–2 hours until firm. Remove. Spread the icing over the top of the chilled base. Refrigerate for a further hour before cutting into triangles with a hot knife.

### ORANGE ICING
Place the sifted icing sugar and butter in a bowl and mix together until the butter is completely crumbed through. Add the orange juice and zest and continue mixing until a smooth paste is formed.

*Makes 24*

OPPOSITE: *above, Dreamy Coconut Triangles; below, Dried Fruit Fingers*

# HEALTHY TREATS

---

*These cookies and bars are crammed full
with nutritious ingredients — and they taste good too!*

## APPLE SHORTCAKE FINGERS

Melting shortcake with a centre of moist, spicy
stewed apple.

*300 g (10 ½ oz, 1 ¼ cups) unsalted butter
300 g (10 ½ oz, 1 ½ cups) caster (superfine) sugar
3 x 60 g (2 oz, large) eggs
300 g (10 ½ oz, 2 ½ cups) plain (all-purpose) flour
1 teaspoon baking powder
1 teaspoon ground cinnamon
1 teaspoon mixed spice (see page 161)
300 g (10 ½ oz, 1 ¼ cups) lightly stewed apple (well drained)
90 g (3 oz, ½ cup) icing (powdered) sugar*

Preheat oven to 180°C (350°F). Lightly grease and
line an 18 cm x 28 cm x 2 cm (7 in x 11 in x ¾ in)
baking tray (sheet) with baking parchment. Cream
the butter and sugar until light and fluffy. Add the
eggs one at a time and continue mixing until well
combined. Sift the flour, baking powder and spices
into the creamed butter and egg mixture and continue mixing until all is well incorporated. Spread
half of this mixture evenly over the base of the tray.
Spread the stewed apple evenly over the base, then
carefully cover the top of the apple with the remaining cake mixture. Bake in the preheated oven
45–55 minutes. Cool in the tray. Dust with icing sugar
and cut into small squares.

*Makes 20*

## PECAN COOKIES

Pecan nuts are a good source of protein, minerals
and vitamins and have no cholesterol. What better
way to enjoy them than in these delicate cookies.

*180 g (6 ½ oz, ¾ cup) unsalted butter
1 tablespoon golden syrup (light treacle)
180 g (6 ½ oz, ¾ cup) caster (superfine) sugar
270 g (9 ½ oz, 2 ¼ cups) plain (all-purpose) flour
1 ½ teaspoons bicarbonate of soda (baking soda)
60 g (2 oz, ½ cup) pecan nuts, chopped
18–24 whole pecan nuts
caster (superfine) sugar, extra, for decorating*

Preheat oven to 180°C (350°F). Line baking trays
(sheets) with baking parchment. Place the butter,
syrup and sugar in a mixing bowl and cream until
light and fluffy. Add the sifted flour, bicarbonate of
soda and chopped pecan nuts and lightly mix to
form a dough. On a lightly floured surface, roll the
dough as thinly as possible and cut into 4 cm (1 ½
in) strips vertically. Then cut 4 cm (1 ½ in) strips
diagonally so that you have cut diamond shapes.
Press a whole pecan nut into the top of each
diamond shape and place it onto the prepared tray.
Bake in the preheated oven 8–10 minutes. Remove
from oven and sprinkle with caster sugar. Cool on
the tray.

*Makes 24*

OPPOSITE: *above, Apple Shortcake Fingers; below, Pecan Cookies*

# GOLDEN OAT FINGERS

*This bar should be stored in the refrigerator 48 hours before cutting into fingers.*

*150 g (5 ½ oz, 1 ¼ cups) plain (all-purpose) flour*
*1 teaspoon baking powder*
*175 g (6 oz, 2 cups) rolled oats*
*225 ml (8 fl oz, 1 cup) olive oil*
*175 g (6 oz, ½ cup) golden syrup (light treacle)*
*175 g (6 oz, ¾ cup) raw cane sugar*
*1 x 60 g (2 oz, large) egg*
*100 ml (3 ½ fl oz, ½ cup) milk*

Preheat oven to 180°C (350°F). Grease and line a 19 cm x 25 cm x 2 cm (7 ½ in x 10 in x ¾ in) baking tray (sheet) with baking parchment.

Place the flour, baking powder and oats in a bowl. Gently warm the oil, golden syrup and raw sugar in a saucepan. Beat the egg with the milk. Pour the syrup mixture and the egg mixture over the dry ingredients and stir together. Beat well for 1–2 minutes.

Pour into the prepared tray and bake in the preheated oven for 1 hour or until firm to touch. Cool on a wire rack. Store for 48 hours in the refrigerator before cutting into fingers.

*Makes 16–20*

# CARROT COOKIES

*Carrots were more popular in sweet dishes than savoury in sixteenth century England. Today we are rediscovering the sweet potential of this vegetable.*

*180 g (6 ½ oz, ¾ cup) salted butter*
*375 g (13 oz, 1 ¾ cups) caster (superfine) sugar*
*juice and zest of 1 lemon*
*3 x 60 g (2 oz, large) eggs*
*120 g (4 oz, 1 cup) carrot, finely grated*
*150 g (5 ½ oz, 1 cup) raisins*
*1 teaspoon baking powder*
*375 g (13 oz, 3 cups) plain (all-purpose) flour*
*icing (powdered) sugar, for dusting*

Preheat oven to 180°C (350°F). Line baking trays (sheets) with baking parchment.

Place the butter, sugar and lemon juice and zest in a mixing bowl and cream together until light and fluffy. Add the eggs slowly and continue to whip until all ingredients are well combined. Add the carrots and raisins and fold through by hand. Sift the baking powder and flour together and add to the mixture, stirring well to ensure the mixture is fully combined.

Place tablespoonfuls of the mixture onto the prepared trays. Bake in the preheated oven 10–12 minutes or until golden brown. Cool on the tray and dust with icing sugar before serving.

*Makes 36*

OPPOSITE: *above, Carrot Cookies; below, Golden Oat Fingers*

# SCOTCH PARKIN FINGERS

*These squares are delicious lightly buttered.*

150 g (5 ½ oz, ⅔ cup) unsalted butter
210 g (7 ½ oz, ⅔ cup) golden syrup (light treacle)
1 tablespoon clear honey
90 g (3 oz, ½ cup) soft (light) brown sugar
75 g (2 ½ oz, ¼ cup) caster (superfine) sugar
1 tablespoon mixed spice (see page 161)
240 g (8 ½ oz, 2 cups) wholemeal (wholegrain) flour
60 g (2 oz, ½ cup) plain (all-purpose) flour
360 g (12 ½ oz, 4 cups) rolled oats
1 ½ teaspoons bicarbonate of soda (baking soda)
200 ml (7 fl oz, 1 cup) milk

Preheat oven to 175°C (345°F). Grease and line an 18 cm x 28 cm x 2 cm (7 in x 11 in x ¾ in) baking tray (sheet) with baking parchment.

Place the butter, golden syrup, honey, brown sugar, caster sugar and spices in a saucepan and place over a low heat. Bring to the boil, stirring continuously so as not to burn the base. Place the flour, oats and bicarbonate of soda in a large mixing bowl and pour the hot liquid over. Using a wooden spoon stir the mixtures together and at the same time begin adding the milk. Stir to a batter.

Pour into the prepared tray. Bake in the preheated oven 45–50 minutes or until firm to the touch. Cool in the tray before cutting into fingers.

*Makes 24*

# WHOLEMEAL FINGERS

Oats are easily the most nutritious of the cereal grasses and are a good source of vitamins B1, B2 and E. Enjoy them in these tasty fingers.

150 g (5 ½ oz, 1 ¼ cups) wholemeal (wholegrain) flour
150 g (5 ½ oz, ⅔ cup) raw cane sugar
150 g (5 ½ oz, 1 ¾ cups) rolled oats
60 g (2 oz, ⅔ cup) desiccated (shredded) coconut
1 teaspoon ground cinnamon
120 g (4 oz, ½ cup) unsalted butter
3 tablespoons boiling water
1 tablespoon golden syrup (light treacle)
1 teaspoon bicarbonate of soda (baking soda)

Preheat oven to 180°C (350°F). Lightly grease and line a 25 cm x 30 cm x 3 cm (10 in x 12 in x 1 ¼ in) baking tray (sheet) with baking parchment.

In a large mixing bowl place the wholemeal flour, sugar, oats, coconut and cinnamon. Place the butter, boiling water and golden syrup in a saucepan and bring to the boil. Stir in the bicarbonate of soda. Pour the mixture over the dry ingredients and stir until thoroughly mixed.

Press the mixture into the prepared tray and using a large knife score the top of the flattened mixture into finger-shaped portions. Bake in the preheated oven 20–25 minutes or until light golden brown. Cool in the tray and then cut into the marked portions.

*Makes 24–30*

OPPOSITE: *above, Scotch Parkin Fingers; below, Wholemeal Fingers*

# SAVOURY TREATS

*Savoury biscuits and cookies are wonderful when entertaining — barbecues, dinner parties or for any special occasion.*

## CHEESE PUFFS

*Superb for pre-dinner drinks or as an hors d'oeuvre, these Cheese Puffs can be made well in advance and frozen until required. To rejuvenate puffs, heat for 20–30 minutes in a slow oven.*

*480 g (16 ½ oz, 4 cups) mild cheese, grated*
*2 x 60 g (2 oz, large) eggs, lightly beaten*
*130 g (4 ½ oz, 1 cup) plain (all-purpose) flour*
*6 teaspoons baking powder*
*2 tablespoons chopped fresh herbs*

Preheat oven to 180°C (350°F). Lightly grease baking trays (sheets).

In a mixing bowl, combine the cheese, eggs, flour and baking powder together with the herbs. Taking small dessertspoonfuls at a time, roll the mixture into a ball and place onto the prepared tray.

Bake in the preheated oven 10–12 minutes or until golden brown.

*Makes 36*

## WATER CRACKERS

*Water crackers are wonderful with dips, cheese and pâté as their subtle flavour never overwhelms.*

*480 g (16 ½ oz, 3 ¾ cups) plain (all-purpose) flour*
*45 g (1 ½ oz, 3 tablespoons) poppy seeds*
*60 g (2 oz, ¼ cup) butter*
*250 ml (9 fl oz, 1 cup) milk*

Preheat oven to 180°C (350°F). Lightly grease baking trays (sheets). Place the flour and poppy seeds in a bowl together and rub through the butter until the mixture resembles coarse breadcrumbs. Add the milk and mix through until a soft but not sticky dough is formed. (If the dough is too stiff add a little more milk; if the dough is too sticky add a little flour.) Knead for 4–5 minutes or until the dough is smooth. Cover with plastic (cling) wrap and set aside for 5 minutes.

Roll the dough out on a lightly floured surface as thinly as possible. Cut into 4 cm (1 ½ in) squares or rounds using a plain cookie cutter. Place the crackers onto the prepared tray and bake in the preheated oven 10–12 minutes or until the crackers are a light golden brown around the edges. Cool on the trays. When cold, wrap immediately in plastic (cling) wrap in batches of 12 and store in an airtight container until required.

*Makes 36*

OPPOSITE: *above, Cheese Puffs; below, Water Crackers*

# CHEESE NUT COOKIES

*Walnuts are said to cure and ward off disease. Whether true or false they give a wonderful flavour to these cookies.*

*240 g (8 ½ oz, 2 cups) mature cheese, grated*
*90 g (3 oz, ⅓ cup) unsalted butter*
*125 ml (4 ½ fl oz, ½ cup) milk*
*150 g (5 ½ oz, 1 ¼ cups) plain (all-purpose) flour*
*120 g (4 oz, 1 cup) walnuts, chopped*

Preheat oven to 180°C (350°F). Line baking trays (sheets) with baking parchment.

Place all ingredients in a bowl and rub through the butter with your fingers. Continue mixing together until a dough is formed. Take teaspoonfuls of the mixture at a time and roll them into balls. Place onto the prepared trays and flatten slightly.

Bake in the preheated oven 8–10 minutes or until golden brown. Cool on the trays before serving warm.

*Makes 24*

# SESAME CRACKERS

*Sesame seeds were introduced to the United States by African slaves. They have since become a staple ingredient in the recipes of the Southern States.*

*480 g (16 ½ oz, 3 ¾ cups) plain (all-purpose) flour*
*75 g (2 ½ oz, ⅓ cup) sesame seeds*
*60 g (2 oz, ¼ cup) salted butter*
*250 ml (9 fl oz, 1 cup) milk*
*2 teaspoons clear honey*
*1 quantity egg wash (see page 156)*
*sesame seeds, extra*

Preheat oven to 180°C (350°F). Lightly grease baking trays (sheets).

Place the flour and sesame seeds into a bowl and crumb through the butter. Add the milk and honey and mix until a dough is formed. (If the dough is too stiff add a little more milk; if the dough is too sticky add a little flour.) Knead for 4–5 minutes or until the dough looks smooth. Cover with plastic (cling) wrap and set aside for 5 minutes. Roll the dough out on a lightly floured surface as thinly as possible. Cut into 4 cm (1 ½ in) squares or rounds using a plain cookie cutter. Place the crackers onto the prepared tray. Glaze with egg wash and sprinkle liberally with extra sesame seeds. Bake in the preheated oven 10–12 minutes or until a light golden brown around the edges. Cool on the trays. When cold, wrap immediately in plastic (cling) wrap in batches of 12 and store in an airtight container until required.

*Makes 48*

OPPOSITE: *above, Sesame Crackers; below, Cheese Nut Cookies*

# SOMETHING SPECIAL

*These recipes are special favourites of mine
— unusual, inventive and delicious.*

## COFFEE CREAM SLICES

Three *different chocolates decorate these slices.*

150 g (5 ¹/₂ oz, ²/₃ cup) unsalted butter
60 g (2 oz, ¹/₄ cup) caster (superfine) sugar
3 tablespoons powdered drinking chocolate, mixed with
sufficient hot water to make a thin paste
2 teaspoons instant coffee granules, mixed with 1 tablespoon
boiling water
4 x 60 g (2 oz, large) egg yolks
6 x 60 g (2 oz, large) egg whites
120 g (4 oz, ¹/₂ cup) caster (superfine) sugar, extra
60 g (2 oz, ¹/₂ cup) plain (all-purpose) flour
45 g (1 ¹/₂ oz, 5 tablespoons) cornflour (US cornstarch)
300 g (10 ¹/₂ oz) dark (plain or semi-sweet) chocolate, melted
120 g (4 oz) white chocolate, melted
120 g (4 oz) milk chocolate, melted
1 quantity chocolate no fuss buttercream (see page 154)

Preheat oven to 180°C (350°F). Line four 20 cm x 30 cm (8 in x 12 in) baking trays (sheets) with baking parchment. Beat the butter, sugar, drinking chocolate and coffee pastes together until the mix is light and fluffy. Add the egg yolks slowly until well combined. Whisk the egg whites until stiff peaks form and then slowly add the extra sugar and continue whisking until all is dissolved. Fold the flour and cornflour into the egg whites and then fold the egg white mixture into the butter mix. Divide the cake mixture equally between the four trays and spread thinly. Bake each tray in the preheated oven 12–15 minutes or until the top springs back when lightly touched. Remove from trays and cool on wire racks. Remove the baking paper from each layer of cake. Place one layer onto a flat surface and spread evenly

with one third of the butter cream, then place another layer on top. Repeat for all layers. Drizzle the dark chocolate over the top layer. Then drizzle the white and milk chocolates over the top layer as well. Allow the chocolate to set before cutting into slices.

*Makes 20*

## PASSIONFRUIT SHORTBREADS

Passionfruit *gives an exotic flavour to traditional shortbread in this recipe.*

360 g (12 ¹/₂ oz, 1 ¹/₂ cups) unsalted butter
120 g (4 oz, ¹/₂ cup) caster (superfine) sugar
360 g (12 ¹/₂ oz, 3 cups) plain (all-purpose) flour
120 g (4 oz, 1 cup) cornflour (US cornstarch)
pulp of 2 passionfruit (purple granadilla)
icing (powdered) sugar, for dusting

Preheat oven to 180°C (350°F). Line baking trays (sheets) with baking parchment. Place the butter and sugar in a mixing bowl and cream together until light, fluffy and almost white. Sift together the flour and cornflour and add this to the well creamed butter. Ensure that the sides of the mixing bowl are scraped down and that all the butter is mixed into the flour. Last add the passionfruit pulp. When well combined but not overmixed, place the mixture in a piping (pastry) bag fitted with a 1 cm (¹/₂ in) star-shaped nozzle. Pipe shell or scallop shapes onto the prepared tray. Bake in the preheated oven 8–10 minutes or until golden brown around the edges. Remove from the oven and dust with icing sugar.

*Makes 36*

OPPOSITE: *above, Coffee Cream Slices; below, Passionfruit Shortbreads*

# TRAFFIC LIGHTS

*A wonderful school holiday treat. Get the children to help you make them.*

*300 g (10 ½ oz, 2 ½ cups) plain (all-purpose) flour*
*150 g (5 ½ oz, 1 cup) icing (powdered) sugar*
*30 g (1 oz, ¼ cup) ground almonds*
*150 g (5 ½ oz, ⅔ cup) unsalted butter*
*1 x 60 g (2 oz, large) egg, lightly beaten*
*1 tablespoon water*

*icing (powdered) sugar, extra, for dusting*
*420 g (15 oz, 1 ¼ cups) apricot jam*
*210 g (7 ½ oz, ⅔ cup) raspberry jam*
*1–2 drops green food colouring*

Line baking trays (sheets) with baking parchment. Place the flour, icing sugar, almonds and butter into a bowl and lightly crumb the butter through the other ingredients until the mixture resembles coarse breadcrumbs. Add the egg and water and work the mixture to a dough. Wrap the dough in plastic (cling) wrap and place in the refrigerator for 30 minutes.

Preheat oven to 180°C (350°F). Remove the dough from the refrigerator and knead until it is ready to roll. Roll on a lightly floured surface as thinly as possible. Using a sharp knife and a ruler cut the dough into rectangles 3 cm x 6 cm (1 in x 2 in). Two rectangles are required for each traffic light. Place all the rectangles onto the prepared trays. Using a 1 cm (½ in) diameter round cookie cutter cut out three evenly spaced holes down the length of half of the rectangles. These will form the top layer of the traffic lights. Bake in the preheated oven 8–12 minutes or until lightly golden brown. Remove and cool on a wire rack.

### TO ASSEMBLE

Dust the top layers of the traffic lights with icing sugar. Take the remaining rectangles and spread each thinly with apricot jam. Have piping (pastry) bags ready. Fill one with raspberry jam, one with half of the apricot jam and one with the remaining apricot jam colored with the green food colouring. Place the top layers on the jam-covered bases and press them together to join. Pipe a different coloured jam into each hole, ensuring the apricot jam is always piped into the centre hole.

*Makes 18*

**STEP ONE:** *Spread half of the rectangles with apricot jam.*

**STEP TWO:** *Place the sugar dusted cookies on top of the jam covered cookies and press together.*

**STEP THREE:** *Pipe a different colored jam into each hole.*

# SWEET AND SOUR COOKIES

*Not to be confused with Chinese take-away! It is the sour cream in this recipe which gives such a rich, tangy flavour.*

*210 g (7 ½ oz, 1 cup) unsalted butter*
*180 g (6 ½ oz, ¾ cup) caster (superfine) sugar*
*1 x 60 g (2 oz, large) egg*
*75 ml (3 fl oz, ⅓ cup) sour cream*
*zest of 1 lemon*
*360 g (12 ½ oz, 3 cups) plain (all-purpose) flour*
*1 ½ teaspoons baking powder*
*icing (powdered) sugar for dusting*

Place the butter in a mixing bowl and beat until light, white and fluffy. And the sugar and cream the mixture for a further 2–3 minutes. Add the egg and mix until well combined. Add the sour cream, lemon zest and sifted flour and baking powder to the mixture and mix until all ingredients are combined into a dough. Wrap the dough in plastic (cling) wrap and refrigerate for 1 hour.

Preheat oven to 180°C (350°F). Lightly grease baking trays (sheets). Remove the dough from the refrigerator and knead lightly on a floured surface to ensure that the mixture will roll easily. Roll out as thinly as possible. Cut the dough with plain or fancy cookie cutters and place onto the prepared tray. Bake in the preheated oven 8–10 minutes or until lightly golden brown. Cool on the tray for 5 minutes and then remove to a wire rack. Dust heavily with icing sugar before serving.

*Makes 36*

# BITTER ORANGE SLICES

*Made without flour, this recipe uses the entire orange — not just the zest and juice — to give it rich, full-bodied flavour.*

*2 whole oranges*
*4 x 60 g (2 oz, large) egg yolks*
*90 g (3 oz, ⅓ cup) caster (superfine) sugar*
*4 x 60 g (2 oz, large) egg whites*
*150 g (5 oz, 1 ⅓ cups) ground almonds*
*1 teaspoon baking powder*
*1 quantity of orange buttercream (see page 154)*
*20–24 orange segments*
*icing (powdered) sugar, for dusting*

Place the oranges in a saucepan. Cover them with water and bring to the boil. Boil for 1 ½ hours. Remove the oranges from the water while hot. Blend to a pulp in a food processor or blender.

Preheat oven to 180°C (350°F). Grease and line a 25 cm x 30 cm x 3 cm (10 in x 12 in x 1 ¼ in) baking tray (sheet) with baking parch-ment. Beat the egg yolks with half of the sugar until the ribbon stage (see page 159). In a separate bowl, beat the egg whites until stiff peaks form (see page 159). Gradually beat in the remaining sugar a spoonful at a time until it is dissolved. Add the ground almonds and baking powder slowly to the meringue and fold through lightly until well combined. Fold the egg yolk mixture into the orange pulp and then fold this mixture through the meringue/almond mixture. Pour into the prepared tray and bake in the preheated oven 30–35 minutes or until firm to the touch. Cool in the tray on a wire rack. When cold, decorate with orange buttercream and orange segments. Dust lightly with icing sugar to bring out the juices of the segments and to keep them fresh. Cut into slices.

*Makes 20–24*

OPPOSITE: *above, Sweet and Sour Cookies; below, Bitter Orange Slices*

# JAFFA RINGS

The perfect marriage of chocolate and orange.

210 g (7 ½ oz, 1 cup) unsalted butter
90 g (3 oz, ½ cup) icing (powdered) sugar
zest of 2 oranges
30 g (1 oz, ¼ cup) cocoa powder
90 g (3 oz) marzipan (see page 160)
1 x 60 g (2 oz, large) egg
240 g (8 ½ oz, 2 cups) plain (all-purpose) flour, sifted
120 g (4 oz) white chocolate, melted (see page 160)

Preheat oven to 180°C (350°F). Line baking trays (sheets) with baking parchment. Place the butter, icing sugar, orange zest, cocoa and marzipan in a mixing bowl and cream together until light and fluffy. Add the egg and mix well. Add the sifted flour and mix until all ingredients are thoroughly combined. Place the mixture into a piping (pastry) bag fitted with a 1 cm (½ in) plain nozzle. Pipe rings of approximately 8 cm (3 in) in diameter onto the prepared trays. Bake in the preheated oven 10 minutes then remove and cool on the trays. When cold drizzle the rings with melted chocolate.

*Makes 18*

# CHOCOLATE COFFEE SHORTCAKES

Shortcake is American in origin, and is a biscuit-like cake.

90 g (3 oz, ¾ cup) cocoa powder
30 g (1 oz, ½ cup) instant coffee granules
150 g (5 ½ oz, 1 ¼ cups) plain (all-purpose) flour
90 g (3 oz, ⅓ cup) caster (superfine) sugar
1 ½ teaspoons baking powder
1 ½ teaspoons bicarbonate of soda (baking soda)
90 g (3 oz, ⅓ cup) butter
125 ml (4 fl oz, ½ cup) thickened (double or heavy) cream
1 x 60 g (2 oz) egg
210 g (7 ½ oz) milk chocolate, melted, for decorating

Preheat oven to 220°C (425°F). Line baking trays (sheets) with baking parchment. Sift all the dry ingredients into a bowl. Add the butter and rub through until mixture resembles fresh breadcrumbs. Add the cream and mix until well combined. Add the egg and mix well. Drop tablespoons of the mixture onto the prepared trays and bake in the preheated oven 10–12 minutes or until cooked. Cool on wire racks and when cold drizzle melted chocolate over the top of each cookie. Allow to set before serving.

*Makes 12*

# ORANGE COCONUT FINGERS

Grand Marnier provides a touch of sophistication to these fingers.

120 g (4 oz, ½ cup) unsalted butter
zest of 2 oranges
240 g (8 ½ oz, 1 ¼ cups) caster (superfine) sugar
4 x 60 g (2 oz, large) eggs
150 g (5 ½ oz, 1 ¼ cups) plain (all-purpose) flour
1 teaspoon baking powder
180 g (6 ½ oz, 2 cups) desiccated (shredded) coconut

SYRUP
50 ml (2 fl oz, ¼ cup) Grand Marnier or orange liqueur
juice of 2 oranges
30 g (1 oz, 2 tablespoons) icing (powdered) sugar

Preheat oven to 160°C (320°F). Grease and line an 18 cm x 28 cm x 2 cm (7 in x 11 in x ¾ in) baking tray (sheet) with baking parchment. Place the butter, orange zest and sugar in a mixing bowl and cream until light and fluffy. Add the eggs one at a time and beat well between additions. Add the sifted flour, baking powder and coconut to the creamed mixure. Stir until all is incorporated. Spread mixture evenly over the prepared tray and bake in the preheated oven 35–40 minutes or until firm to touch. Remove tray from oven and immediately brush over the syrup. Allow to cool before cutting into portions using a sharp serrated knife.

SYRUP
Mix the Grand Marnier and orange juice together. Whisk in the icing sugar until all lumps have dissolved.

*Makes 24*

OPPOSITE: *above, Orange Coconut Fingers; centre, Jaffa Rings; below, Chocolate Coffee Shortcakes*

# PERNOD SABLE

*Pernod is an aniseed-flavoured liqueur.*

225 g (8 ½ oz, 1 cup) unsalted butter
115 g (4 oz, ½ cup) caster (superfine) sugar
1 x 60 g (2 oz, large) egg yolk
2 tablespoons Pernod
270 g (9 ½ oz, 2 ¼ cups) plain (all-purpose) flour
1 teaspoon baking powder
30–36 blanched almonds, whole
icing (powdered) sugar, for dusting

Cream the butter and sugar until light, fluffy and pale in colour. Add the egg yolk and Pernod and mix well. Add the sifted flour and baking powder and combine until all ingredients are well mixed. Wrap the dough in plastic (cling) wrap and refrigerate for 1 hour.

Preheat oven to 175°C (345°F). Line baking trays (sheets) with baking parchment. Remove the dough from the refrigerator and roll out on a lightly floured surface to 5 mm (⅕ in) in thickness. Cut out shapes using a tear drop or oval cookie cutter. In the centre of each Sablé press a whole almond. Place onto the prepared tray. Bake in the preheated oven 8–10 minutes. Cool on the tray before serving.

*Makes 30–36*

# FLAMING HEARTS

*You may need a few practice sessions with this recipe until you manage to pipe the heart so that it retains its shape when baked.*

330 g (11 ½ oz, 1 ⅓ cups) unsalted butter
180 g (6 ½ oz, 1 cup) icing (powdered) sugar, sifted
1 x 60 g (2 oz, large) egg
330 g (11 ½ oz, 2 ¾ cups) plain (all-purpose) flour
1 tablespoon ground cinnamon
240 g (8 ½ oz, 2 ¼ cups) ground hazelnuts
vanilla essence (extract), to taste

### WATER ICING
420 g (14 oz, 2 ½ cups ) icing (powdered) sugar
warm water

Preheat oven to 180°C (350°F). Line baking trays (sheets) with baking parchment. Cream the butter and sugar in a mixing bowl until light and fluffy. Add the egg and vanilla and mix well. Sift the flour and add to the cake crumbs, cinnamon and ground hazelnuts. Add the dry ingredients to the creamed mixture. Mix until well combined. Place the mixture into a large piping (pastry) bag fitted with a 1 ½ cm (½ in) star-shaped nozzle. Pipe heart shapes onto the prepared tray, allowing room for spreading. Bake in the preheated oven 12–15 minutes or until cooked. Remove from oven and cool slightly before brushing lightly with water icing.

### WATER ICING
Mix the icing sugar with sufficient water to make an icing thick enough to leave a trail when it is swirled over itself. It has to remain thin enough to spread.

*Makes 36*

OPPOSITE: *above, Flaming Hearts; below, Pernod Sablé*

# MOCCA SUPREME

*A pastry base covered with melt-in-the-mouth honey filling and crowned with streusel — heaven!*

### BASE
*120 g (4 oz, ½ cup) unsalted butter*
*75 g (2 ½ oz, ⅓ cup) icing (powdered) sugar*
*150 g (5 ½ oz, 1 ¼ cups) plain (all-purpose) flour*
*1 x 60 g (2 oz) egg yolk*

### FILLING
*800 ml (27 fl oz, 3 ½ cups) sweetened condensed milk*
*75 g (2 ½ oz, ¼ cup) unsalted butter*
*1 tablespoon golden syrup (light treacle)*
*1 tablespoon clear honey*
*30 g (1 oz, ¼ cup) powdered drinking chocolate, dissolved in*
*15 ml ( ½ fl oz, 1 tablespoon) boiling water*

### TOPPING
*120 g (4 oz, 1 cup) plain (all-purpose) flour*
*120 g (4 oz, ½ cup) unsalted butter*
*90 g (3 oz, ⅓ cup) caster (superfine) sugar*
*90 g (3 oz, ¾ cup) ground almonds*
*1 teaspoon ground cinnamon*

*icing (powdered) sugar, extra*

Preheat oven to 180°C (350°F). Grease and line an 18 cm x 28 cm x 2 cm (7 in x 11 in x ¾ in) baking tray (sheet) with baking parchment.

### BASE
Place all the ingredients in a mixing bowl and beat until soft. Press the mixture onto the base of the prepared tray and bake in the preheated oven 8–10 minutes or until lightly golden brown.

### FILLING
Place the condensed milk, butter, golden syrup, honey and drinking chocolate mixed with the water in a saucepan and slowly bring to the boil, stirring continuously. Continue to boil for a further 2–4 minutes or until the mixture becomes quite thick, stirring constantly. Do not allow the mixture to catch on the base of the pan. Pour over the precooked base and spread smooth.

### TOPPING
Place all ingredients in a mixing bowl and rub the butter through until the mixture resembles fresh breadcrumbs. Continue mixing by hand until the mixture forms into large balls.

### TO FINISH
Sprinkle the topping over the filling and bake for 15 minutes in the preheated oven. Remove from the oven and cool in the tray for 2 hours. Dust with icing sugar and cut into small squares.

*Makes 20*

# COFFEE FORCER COOKIES

*'Forced' or piped into a rosette, these cookies make an attractive dinner party treat with coffee.*

*180 g (6 ½ oz, ¾ cup) unsalted butter, softened*
*120 g (4 oz, ½ cup) caster (superfine) sugar*
*15 g ( ½ oz, 3 tablespoons) instant coffee granules*
*1 teaspoon boiling water*
*1 x 60 g (2 oz, large) egg yolk*
*210 g (7 ½ oz, 1 ¾ cups) plain (all-purpose) flour*
*15 g ( ½ oz, 2 tablespoons) cocoa powder*
*1 teaspoon baking powder*
*icing (powdered) sugar, for dusting*

Preheat oven to 180°C (350°F). Line baking trays (sheets) with baking parchment. Place the softened butter and caster sugar in a mixing bowl and beat together until light and fluffy. Dissolve the coffee in the boiling water. When the butter is whipped, add the coffee mixture and the egg yolk and mix thoroughly. Add the sifted flour, cocoa powder and baking powder. Beat until combined. Do not overmix and ensure that the mixing bowl is scraped down and all ingredients are well incorporated. Place the mixture into a piping (pastry) bag fitted with a large 1–2 cm (½–1 in) star-shaped nozzle. Pipe the mixture in rosettes onto the prepared tray. Bake in the preheated oven 8–10 minutes. Cool on the tray and dust lightly with icing sugar before serving.

*Makes 18*

OPPOSITE: *above, Mocca Supreme; below, Coffee Forcer Cookies*

# CHOCOLATE PRETZELS

*Practice makes perfect when it comes to twisting a pretzel.*

*28 ml (1 fl oz, 2 tablespoons) boiling water*
*30 g (1 oz, ¼ cup) cocoa powder*
*120 g (4 oz, ½ cup) unsalted butter*
*60 g (2 oz, ¼ cup) caster (superfine) sugar*
*1 x 60 g (2 oz, large) egg*
*½ teaspoon vanilla essence (extract)*
*240 g (8 ½ oz, 2 cups) plain (all-purpose) flour*
*390 g (14 oz) dark (plain or semi-sweet) chocolate, melted*
*(see page 160)*

Place the boiling water in a cup and stir in the cocoa powder until a smooth paste is formed. Place the butter and sugar in a bowl and cream together until the mixture is light and fluffy. Add the egg and mix until well combined. Add the vanilla and cocoa paste to the creamed mixture and mix until all ingredients are combined. Sift the flour and add to the mixture. Work to a soft dough. Wrap in plastic (cling) wrap and place in the refrigerator for 1 hour.

Preheat oven to 170°C (340°F). Line baking trays (sheets) with baking parchment. Lightly knead the chilled dough so that it is soft enough to roll by hand. Taking small amounts of the dough at a time, roll sausage shapes ½ cm x 15 cm (¼ in x 6 in). Place onto the prepared tray and lay flat. Taking both ends in your hands, draw them up towards you so that each end meets in the middle. Cross the two ends over each other and then draw them back through the loops to form a pretzel. Continue until all the dough is used. Bake in the preheated oven 8–10 minutes. Cool on the tray. Dip the cold pretzels in the melted chocolateand place on a wire rack to drain before returning them to the lined tray to set in the refrigerator.

*Makes 18*

**STEP ONE:** *Take both ends of the sausage shape and draw them up towards you so that each end meets in the middle.*

**STEP TWO:** *Cross the two ends over each other.*

**STEP THREE:** *Draw them back into the base of the shape.*

# SPICE SLICES

*This recipe is a great way to make use of leftover cake.*

210 g (7 ¹⁄₂ oz, 2 cups) cake crumbs
100 ml (3 ¹⁄₂ fl oz, ¹⁄₂ cup) milk
180 g (6 ¹⁄₂ oz, ³⁄₄ cup) unsalted butter, softened
120 g (4 oz, ¹⁄₂ cup) caster (superfine) sugar
4 x 60 g (2 oz, large) eggs
240 g (8 ¹⁄₂ oz, 2 cups) plain (all-purpose) flour
1 tablespoon baking powder
15 g ( ¹⁄₂ oz, 2 tablespoons) cocoa powder
15 g ( ¹⁄₂ oz, 6 teaspoons) ground ginger
15 g ( ¹⁄₂ oz, 6 teaspoons) ground cinnamon
60 g (2 oz, 2 tablespoons) clear honey
500 g (17 ¹⁄₂ oz, 1 ¹⁄₂ cups) apricot jam
210 g (7 ¹⁄₂ oz) dark (plain or semi-sweet) chocolate, melted
(see page 160)

Preheat oven to 175°C (345°F). Grease an 18 cm x 28 cm x 2 cm (7 in x 11 in x ¾ in) baking tray (sheet). Place the cake crumbs in a bowl. Add the milk and allow the cake crumbs to soak. Place the softened butter and sugar in a bowl and cream them together until light, fluffy and pale in colour. Add the eggs gradually to the creamed mixture and beat well after each addition. Sift the flour, baking powder, cocoa, ginger and cinnamon and add to the creamed mixture. Add the honey and stir all ingredients until a smooth batter is formed. Add the soaked cake crumbs and stir to combine thoroughly. Pour the mixture into the prepared tray and level out using a spatula or palette knife.

Bake in the preheated oven 30–35 minutes or until a skewer inserted in the centre comes out clean. Cool in the tray on a wire rack. When cool, cut into three layers horizontally and spread each layer with apricot jam. Stack each layer on top of each other. Place the remaining jam in a saucepan and bring to the boil. Boil until thick and dark in colour (3–5 minutes). Using a pastry brush, brush the apricot jam evenly over the top of the slice. Melt the chocolate in a double boiler and then pour over the top of the apricot jam. Spread evenly and just as it is about to set, score the chocolate into serving portions with a hot knife to make it easier to cut when cold.

*Makes 25–30*

# AMAREE COOKIES

*My own creation and filled with my favourite things — spices and chocolate.*

180 g (6 oz, ³⁄₄ cup) unsalted butter, softened
180 g (6 oz, 1 cup) soft (light) brown sugar
80 g (2 ¹⁄₂ oz, ¹⁄₄ cup) golden syrup (light treacle)
1 x 60 g (2 oz, large) egg
250 g (8 ¹⁄₂ oz, 2 cups) plain (all-purpose) flour
2 teaspoons baking powder
2 tablespoons cocoa powder
2 teaspoons ground cinnamon
raw cane sugar for coating
200 g (7 oz) dark (plain or semi-sweet) chocolate, melted
(see page 160)
200 g (7 oz, 1 ¹⁄₄ cups) roasted sesame seeds

Place the butter, sugar and golden syrup in a mixing bowl and cream until light and fluffy. Add the egg and mix until combined. Sift the flour, baking powder, cocoa and cinnamon together and add in two batches to the creamed mixture. Mix well. Cover with plastic (cling) wrap and refrigerate for 45 minutes.

Preheat oven to 180°C(350°F). Line baking trays (sheets) with baking parchment. Remove the mixture from the refrigerator. Take walnut-sized portions and roll into a ball. Dip half of the ball into the raw sugar and place on the prepared tray. Allow at least 5 cm (2 in) between each cookie for spreading. Bake in the preheated oven 10–12 minutes. Remove from the oven and allow to coool slightly on the tray before placing on a wire rack. When the cookies are cool, dip the bases lightly in chocolate and then in the sesame seeds. Place on a tray to set.

*Makes 24*

OPPOSITE: *above, Amaree Cookies; below, Spice Squares*

# ROSE PETAL COOKIES

*Make sure you use unsprayed rose petals for this recipe.*

**120 g (4 oz, ¾ cup) icing (powdered) sugar**
**255 g (9 oz, 1 ¾ cups) plain (all-purpose) flour**
**200 g (7 oz, 1 cup) unsalted butter**
**petals of 2 red or yellow perfumed roses**
**zest of 1 lemon**

Sift the icing sugar and flour together and place in a bowl. Cut the butter and the rose petals into small pieces and lightly rub through the dry ingredients until the mixture resembles fine breadcrumbs. Add the lemon zest and continue to blend the mixture with the fingers until it forms a solid or heavy dough. Remove from the bowl, and lightly knead into a ball shape.

Place the mixture in the centre of a sheet of baking parchment paper and fold both ends of the paper over to meet on one side so that the dough is enclosed in the centre and the ends are open. While holding the bottom piece of paper with one hand, use the other hand to press a plastic dough scraper firmly into the base of the pastry until the mixture tightens and forms a roll. Wrap completely in the baking parchment and place in the refrigerator for 1 hour.

Preheat oven to 175°C (345°F). Line baking trays (sheets) with baking parchment. Remove the dough from the refrigerator and cut into very thin slices. Place each disc onto the prepared tray. Bake in the preheated oven 8–10 minutes or until very lightly golden brown.

*Makes 24*

**STEP ONE:** *Fold the baking parchment over the dough.*

**STEP TWO:** *Hold the bottom piece of the baking parchment with one hand and with the other, using a plastic dough scraper or spatula, press firmly into the base of the pastry.*

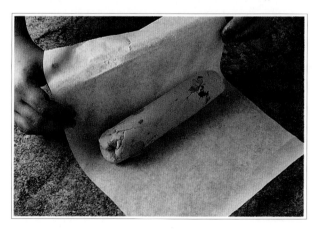

**STEP THREE:** *Continue pressing until the mixture tightens and forms a roll.*

# TOPPINGS *and* FILLINGS

## BUTTERCREAMS

It is best to use buttercream as soon as it is made, when it is light, airy and fresh. If buttercream has to be stored it should be kept in an airtight container in the refrigerator. Remove from the refrigerator when required and stand at room temperature for 1 hour to soften. Beat in a mixing bowl until light and fluffy. Never store for more than two weeks in the refrigerator. Quick No-fuss Buttercream provides the basic recipe for the other buttercreams.

### QUICK NO-FUSS BUTTERCREAM

*250 g (9 oz, 1 cup) unsalted butter*
*90 g (3 oz, ¹/₂ cup) icing (powdered) sugar*
*2 x 60 g (2 oz, large) eggs*
*1 teaspoon vanilla essence (extract)*

Beat the butter and icing sugar together until blended. Add the eggs one at a time, beating well after each addition. Add the vanilla and beat for 15 minutes on medium speed until the mixture is light and creamy.

*Makes 400 g (14 oz)*

## CHOCOLATE BUTTERCREAM

After the butter, icing sugar, eggs and vanilla have been mixed together, blend 100 g (3 ¹/₂ oz) cooled, melted dark (plain or semi-sweet) chocolate to the mixture and beat for 15 minutes at medium speed.

## ORANGE BUTTERCREAM

Add the zest of 1 orange and 1 tablespoon of orange juice to the butter and icing sugar mixture and mix for 5 minutes at medium speed before adding the eggs. Beat for 15 minutes at medium speed. (Pictured on opposite page).

## GANACHE

*200 ml (6 ½ fl oz, ¾ cup) cream (single or light)*
*40 g (1 ½ oz, 2 tablespoons) unsalted butter*
*600 g (21 oz) dark (plain or semi-sweet) chocolate, chopped*

Place the cream and butter in a saucepan and bring to the boil. Add the chocolate and stir until melted.

The ganache can be used immediately to cover a baked base. Place the base on a wire rack and top with ganache. Use a palette knife to smooth the ganache and chill until set.

If the ganache is to be used as a whipped covering, set aside in a cool place to firm before whipping with an electric mixer. The ganache is ready when it has become lighter in colour.

# GLAZES

## FONDANT GLAZE

For the small amounts required it is more convenient to buy fondant. Most large supermarkets and delicatessens stock ready-made fondant in small tubs. If fondant is not available, use water icing.

To melt fondant, place in a small bowl over a pan of simmering water. If it is too stiff to spread easily, add a very small amount of water. Do not heat above 30°C (86°F) or the fondant will crystallise.

To store fondant, keep covered with a thin layer of water or sugar syrup to prevent it forming a skin and drying out.

## APRICOT GLAZE

*300 g (10 ½ oz, ¾ cup) apricot jam*
*60 ml (2 fl oz, 4 tablespoons) water*
*2 teaspoons lemon juice*

Place all the ingredients in a saucepan and stir until thoroughly blended and smooth. Boil for 10–15 minutes. Force through a fine wire strainer. Brush the warm glaze over the baked base or cookie. Allow to cool before decorating.

Store excess glaze in a covered container in the refrigerator. Do not store for more than 3 weeks. (Pictured over page)

*Makes sufficient to cover one 23 cm (9 in) base.*

## EGG WASH

Egg wash gives a glossy sheen to cookies and baked bases and is also used to join and seal layers of pastry before baking.

*1 x 60 g (2 oz, large) egg*
*30 ml (1 fl oz, 2 tablespoons) water*

Lightly beat the egg. Mix in the water. The egg wash is now ready to use. Egg wash can be stored in a covered container in the refrigerator for 2 days.

*Makes approximately 100 ml.*

## SACHER TORTE GLAZE

*250 g (9 oz, 1 ¼ cups) caster (superfine) sugar*
*200 g (7 oz) couverture chocolate, chopped*
*150 ml (5 ½ fl oz, ⅔ cup) water*

Place all the ingredients in a saucepan and slowly bring to the boil.

Boil until the syrup reaches 115°C (240°F), using a sugar (candy) thermometer. Cool slightly and pour over an apricot glazed baked base.

One quantity of this mixture will cover one Sacher bar.

## ICINGS AND FROSTINGS

## ROYAL ICING

Royal Icing dries out easily and must be covered at all times with a slightly damp cloth. If the icing forms a skin or crust, small lumps will block the piping (pastry) nozzle when trying to write.

*1–2 egg whites, at room temperature*
*350 g (12 ¼ oz, 2 cups) icing (powdered) sugar, sifted*
*1–2 drops of acetic acid or lemon juice*

Place the egg whites in small bowl. Add 2 spoonfuls of the icing sugar and beat for 2 minutes by hand or until the mixture is combined. Stir in the acetic acid

or lemon juice a drop at a time, beating well after each addition.

Add enough icing sugar to reach the 'soft peak' stage. (If mixture is too moist add a little more icing sugar until desired consistency is achieved.) When the icing mixture can hold a peak and fold back down (see page 159) the icing is suitable for writing and lattice work.

To store the icing, place it in a plastic bag inside a plastic container to prevent drying out and setting. Do not store for more than 3 days and beat for 5–10 minutes before using.

To cover a baked base with Royal Icing; place a thin layer of rolled marzipan over the base then spread the icing over the top and sides. Royal Icing can be smoothed before decorating or use a palette knife to fleck the icing to form small peaks.

The baked base should be eaten within 2–3 days or the icing will dry out and become hard.

## LEMON/ORANGE FROSTING

*juice and zest of 1 lemon or 1 orange*
*270 g (9 ½ oz, 1 ½ cups) icing (powdered) sugar, sifted*
*1 tablespoon glucose (corn) syrup*
*30 g (1 oz, 6 teaspoons) unsalted butter*

Place the zest, icing sugar, syrup and butter in a mixing bowl and blend together slowly. When ingredients are combined add the juice slowly, stirring all the time. When all ingredients are thoroughly mixed, beat for 15 minutes on top speed or until the frosting is white, light and fluffy.

*Makes sufficient to cover one 23 cm (9 in) baked base.*

## LEMON CREAM CHEESE FROSTING

*240 g (8 oz, 1 ½ cups) icing (powdered) sugar*
*90 g (3 oz, ⅓ cup) cream cheese, softened*
*45 g (1 ½ oz, 3 tablespoons) unsalted butter, softened*
*1 teaspoon vanilla essence (extract)*
*zest and juice of 1 lemon*

Place icing sugar, cream cheese and butter in a mixing bowl and combine. Add the vanilla essence, lemon juice and rind and mix at top speed for 5 minutes or until light and fluffy.

## CHOCOLATE FROSTING

*30 g (1 oz, ¼ cup) cocoa powder*
*240 g (8 oz, 1 ½ cups) icing (powdered) sugar, sifted*
*1 tablespoon glucose (corn) syrup*
*30 g (1 oz, 6 teaspoons) unsalted butter*
*1 tablespoon water*

Place the cocoa powder, icing sugar, syrup and butter in a mixing bowl and blend together slowly. When combined, add the water slowly, beating all the time. When all ingredients are thoroughly mixed, beat for 15 minutes on top speed or until the frosting is light and fluffy.

Note: If the frosting looks as if it has split, add a little more icing sugar.

## ROASTED FLAKED ALMONDS/HAZELNUTS

*250 g (9 oz, 2 ¼ cups) flaked almonds/whole hazelnuts*

Preheat oven to 180°C (350°F). Spread the almonds thinly on a baking tray (sheet). Bake for 4 minutes. Remove the tray and use a fork to turn the almonds. Return to oven and bake for a further 4 minutes. Remove and turn again. Continue this process until the almonds are golden brown. Allow to cool on the tray.

Makes sufficient to cover the sides of one 23 cm (9 in) baked base. Roasted almonds can be stored in an airtight container for up to 2 weeks.

# IMPORTANT NOTES

All ingredients should be at room temperature when used unless the recipe advises otherwise.

Ensure that all utensils are clean, grease free and dry before cooking. Water or grease on utensils can adversely affect recipes, especially when using egg whites which will not achieve maximum aeration if mixed with even small amounts of water or grease.

## CUP MEASUREMENTS

Metric, imperial and cup and spoon conversions are provided for all ingredient quantities. The cup measurement is based on a 250 ml (8 fl oz) cup. This corresponds to a metric cup, however, the British standard cup is 10 oz. Nearest equivalences have been provided, however, the author prefers weighing ingredients for utmost accuracy.

## EGG WHITES

### SOFT PEAKS

Beaten egg whites reach the soft peak stage when the peaks will slowly fold back down on the count of four.

## STIFF PEAKS

The stiff peak stage has been reached when the peaks will hold their shape indefinitely.

## RIBBON STAGE

The 'ribbon stage' of any mixture has been achieved when a dribble from the whisk or spoon will form an impression of itself on top of the mixture and remain there for the count of 8 or indefinitely.

# TO MELT CHOCOLATE

The easiest way to melt chocolate is in a double boiler or in a bowl over simmering water. Break the chocolate into small pieces to speed up the melting process.

Place a saucepan of water over the heat and bring to a simmer. Remove from the heat, place the chocolate into a small glass or stainless steel bowl which fits the saucepan and place the bowl over the hot water.

Never allow the water to come in contact with the bowl and stir the chocolate until it liquefies. Keep the chocolate liquefied while working. Place the bowl over simmering water in cold weather.

Melting or melted chocolate should never be covered as condensed water on the lid can fall back into the chocolate. Even a small amount of water in the melted chocolate will make it thicken and turn into a solid mass.

# MARZIPAN

Also known as almond paste, marzipan is a sweetened mixture of ground almonds, glucose (corn) syrup and icing (powdered) sugar. Marzipan is available in a variety of sizes and packagings, from 200 g (7 oz) rolls to 7 kg (15 ½ lb) boxes and is white or yellow depending on the manufacturer's recipe.

STORAGE: Marzipan can absorb moisture or dry out so careful storage is important. If it absorbs moisture it will begin to dissolve. If marzipan dries out it will begin to ferment.

Wrap in plastic (cling) wrap and place in an airtight container. Store at room temperature in a dark place for up to three weeks.

BAKING WITH MARZIPAN: To bake marzipan it must have a higher proportion of almonds than sugar. If the proportion of sugar is too high, the marzipan will boil instead of bake, which will adversely affect the quality, taste and appearance of the finished biscuits.

# MAKING A PIPING BAG

STEP ONE: *Begin all piping bags with a triangle-shaped piece of baking parchment paper.*

STEP TWO: *Start by taking the top corner of the paper and curling it along the longest edge.*

STEP THREE: *Pinch the point of the curl with one hand and continue curling the paper with the other.*

**STEP FOUR:** *When all of the paper has been rolled tuck the remaining flap inside the cone.*

*Cut a small point from the end of the bag. If a larger opening is required it is best to cut small pieces from the tip until you attain the required size. If too large a tip is cut the filling may escape too easily.*

*The bag is now ready to fill with any mixture and begin piping. Half fill the piping bag for best results.*

# MIXED SPICE

*1 level teaspooon ground cinnamon*
*½ level teaspoon ground ginger*
*¼ level teaspoon ground nutmeg*
*¼ level teaspoon ground cloves*

Combine all dry ingredients in a small mixing bowl.

# OVEN TEMPERATURES AND GAS MARKS

The following tables give the equivalent Numbered Temperature Control Knob Setting for gas ovens. Check the temperature (given in degrees Celsius) in the appropriate table for your oven.

| | |
|---|---|
| 100 degrees C – ¼ | 100 degrees C – 1 |
| 110 degrees C – ½ | 110 degrees C – 2 |
| 120 degrees C – 1 | 120 degrees C – 3 |
| 140 degrees C – 2 | 140 degrees C – 4 |
| 150 degrees C – 3 | 150 degrees C – 5 |
| 160 degrees C – 4 | 160 degrees C – 6 |
| 180 degrees C – 5 | 180 degrees C – 7 |
| 190 degrees C – 6 | 190 degrees C – 8 |
| 200 degrees C – 7 | 200 degrees C – 9 |
| 220 degrees C – 8 | 220 degrees C – 10 |
| 230 degrees C – 9 | 230 degrees C – 11 |

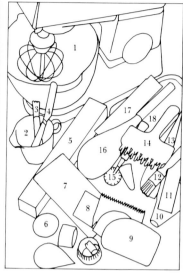

## EQUIPMENT

1. Mixmaster
2. Measuring cup
3. Lemon zester
4. Palette knife
5. Baking parchment
6. Biscuit (cookie) cutters
7. Cooking chocolate
8. Baking powder
9. Dough scraper
10. Piping (pastry) bag
11. Ruler
12. Pastry brush
13. Spatula
14. Docker (used for pricking pastry)
15. Fluted pastry cutter
16. Fine wire whisk
17. Sugar (candy) thermometer
18. Baking tray (sheet)

# INDEX